Perl - A Beginner's Guide

Table of Contents

Adding and Removing Elements in Array: 61

Slicing Array Elements: 64

Replacing Array Elements 65

Transform Strings to Arrays..66

Transform Arrays to Strings: 68

Sorting Arrays: 69

The $[Special Variable: 70

Merging Arrays: 71

Selecting Elements from Lists: 73

Perl – Hashes **75**

Creating Hashes: 77

Accessing Hash Elements: 78

Extracting Slices: 79

Extracting Keys and Values: 79

Checking for Existence: 81

Getting Hash Size: 82

Add and Remove Elements in Hashes: 83

Perl Conditional Statements - IF...ELSE **85**

Perl – Loops **109**

do...while Loop: **126**

Perl – Operators **132**

What is an Operator? 133

Perl Arithmetic Operators: 134

Perl Equality Operators: 138

PERL - A Beginner's Guide

PERL Tutorial for Beginners

Perl stands in for "**Practical Extraction and Reporting Language**" even though there is no authorized acronym for Perl. You may create your own acronym, and no one will mind. Perl was created by **Larry Wall** in 1987 when he was employed on a bug reporting system and "AWK"- a programming language he was using for the purpose was not helping him much. He is still the chief architect and developer of Perl. If we want to define Perl in one sentence: Perl is a high-level, interpreted, dynamic programming language. Did it all sound Greek to you? (Unless you actually know Greek).

Perl is a programming language specially designed for text editing. It is now widely used for a variety of purposes including Linux system administration, network programming, web development, etc.

Let's put it in a simple manner. While computers understand just 0's and 1's (binary language/machine language/ [low-level language]), it is very difficult to program in a binary language for us human. Perl is a programming language which uses natural language elements, words that are used in common English language and is, therefore, easier to understand by humans [**high-level language**]. Now there's a problem; computers cannot understand high-level languages, which we humans can easily understand. For that, we need something which can translate the high-level language to low-level language. Here interpreter comes to our help. The interpreter is a piece of software which converts the program written in the high-level language to low-level language for the computer to understand and execute the instructions written in the program. Hence, Perl is an **interpreted programming language**.

To whom this tutorial is designed for:

This reference has been prepared for beginners to help them understand the basic to advanced concepts related to Perl Scripting languages.

Prerequisites:

Before you start practicing with various types of examples given in this reference, we are making an assumption that you have prior exposure to C programming and Unix Shell.

Perl - Introduction

Perl is a general-purpose programming language originally developed for text manipulation and now used for a wide range of tasks including system administration, web development, network programming, GUI development, and more.

What is Perl?

- Perl is a stable, cross platform programming language.

- Though Perl is not officially an acronym but few people used it as **Practical Extraction and Report Language**.

- It is used for mission critical projects in the public and private sectors.

- Perl is an *Open Source* software, licensed under its *Artistic License*, or the *GNU General Public License (GPL)*.

- Perl was created by Larry Wall.

- Perl 1.0 was released to usenet's alt.comp.sources in 1987.

- At the time of writing this tutorial, the latest version of perl was 5.16.2.

- Perl is listed in the *Oxford English Dictionary*.

PC Magazine announced Perl as the finalist for its 1998 Technical Excellence Award in the Development Tool category.

Perl Features

- Perl takes the best features from other languages, such as C, awk, sed, sh, and BASIC, among others.

- Perls database integration interface DBI supports third-party databases including Oracle, Sybase, Postgres, MySQL and others.

- Perl works with HTML, XML, and other mark-up languages.

- Perl supports Unicode.

- Perl is Y2K compliant.

- Perl supports both procedural and object-oriented programming.

- Perl interfaces with external C/C++ libraries through XS or SWIG.

- Perl is extensible. There are over 20,000 third party modules available from the Comprehensive Perl Archive Network (CPAN).

- The Perl interpreter can be embedded into other systems.

Perl and the Web

- Perl used to be the most popular web programming language due to its text manipulation capabilities and rapid development cycle.

- Perl is widely known as "the duct-tape of the Internet".

- Perl can handle encrypted Web data, including e-commerce transactions.

- Perl can be embedded into web servers to speed up processing by as much as 2000%.

- Perl's mod_perl allows the Apache web server to embed a Perl interpreter.

- Perl's DBI package makes web-database integration easy.

Perl is Interpreted

Perl is an interpreted language, which means that your code can be run as is, without a compilation stage that creates a non portable executable program.

Traditional compilers convert programs into machine language. When you run a Perl program, it's first compiled into a byte code, which is then converted (as the program runs) into machine instructions. So it is not quite the same as shells, or Tcl, which are **strictly** interpreted without an intermediate representation.

It is also not like most versions of C or C++, which are compiled directly into a machine dependent format. It is somewhere in between, along with *Python* and *awk* and Emacs .elc files.

Perl – Environment

Before we start writing our Perl programs, let's understand how to setup our Perl environment. Perl is available on a wide variety of platforms –

- Unix (Solaris, Linux, FreeBSD, AIX, HP/UX, SunOS, IRIX etc.)
- Win 9x/NT/2000/
- WinCE
- Macintosh (PPC, 68K)
- Solaris (x86, SPARC)
- OpenVMS
- Alpha (7.2 and later)
- Symbian
- Debian GNU/kFreeBSD
- MirOS BSD
- And many more...

This is more likely that your system will have perl installed on it. Just try giving the following command at the $ prompt –

```
$perl -v
```

If you have perl installed on your machine, then you will get a message something as follows –

This is perl 5, version 16, subversion 2 (v5.16.2) built for i686-linux

Copyright 1987-2012, Larry Wall

Perl may be copied only under the terms of either the Artistic License or the
GNU General Public License, which may be found in the Perl 5 source kit.

Complete documentation for Perl, including FAQ lists, should be found on
this system using "man perl" or "perldoc perl". If you have access to the
Internet, point your browser at http://www.perl.org/, the Perl Home Page.

If you do not have perl already installed, then proceed to the next section.

Getting Perl Installation

The most up-to-date and current source code, binaries, documentation, news, etc. are available at the official website of Perl.

Perl Official Website – https://www.perl.org/

You can download Perl documentation from the following site.

Perl Documentation Website – https://perldoc.perl.org

Install Perl

Perl distribution is available for a wide variety of platforms. You need to download only the binary code applicable for your platform and install Perl.

If the binary code for your platform is not available, you need a C compiler to compile the source code manually. Compiling the source code offers more flexibility in terms of choice of features that you require in your installation.

Here is a quick overview of installing Perl on various platforms.

Unix and Linux Installation

Here are the simple steps to install Perl on Unix/Linux machine.

- Open a Web browser and go to https://www.perl.org/get.html.

- Follow the link to download zipped source code available for Unix/Linux.

- Download **perl-5.x.y.tar.gz** file and issue the following commands at $ prompt.

```
$tar -xzf perl-5.x.y.tar.gz

$cd perl-5.x.y

$./Configure -de
```

```
$make

$make test

$make install
```

NOTE – Here $ is a Unix prompt where you type your command, so make sure you are not typing $ while typing the above mentioned commands.

This will install Perl in a standard location */usr/local/bin* and its libraries are installed in */usr/local/lib/perlXX*, where XX is the version of Perl that you are using.

It will take a while to compile the source code after issuing the **make** command. Once installation is done, you can issue **perl -v**command at $ prompt to check perl installation. If everything is fine, then it will display message like we have shown above.

Windows Installation

Here are the steps to install Perl on Windows machine.

- Follow the link for the Strawberry Perl installation on Windows http://strawberryperl.com

- Download either 32bit or 64bit version of installation.

- Run the downloaded file by double-clicking it in Windows Explorer. This brings up the Perl install wizard, which is really easy to use. Just accept the default settings, wait until the installation is finished, and you're ready to roll!

Macintosh Installation

In order to build your own version of Perl, you will need 'make', which is part of the Apples developer tools usually supplied with Mac OS install DVDs. You do not need the latest version of Xcode (which is now charged for) in order to install make.

Here are the simple steps to install Perl on Mac OS X machine.

- Open a Web browser and go to https://www.perl.org/get.html.

- Follow the link to download zipped source code available for Mac OS X.

- Download **perl-5.x.y.tar.gz** file and issue the following commands at $ prompt.

```
$tar -xzf perl-5.x.y.tar.gz

$cd perl-5.x.y

$./Configure -de
```

```
$make

$make test

$make install
```

This will install Perl in a standard location */usr/local/bin* and its libraries are installed in */usr/local/lib/perlXX*, where XX is the version of Perl that you are using.

Running Perl

The following are the different ways to start Perl.

Interactive Interpreter:

You can enter **perl** and start coding right away in the interactive interpreter by starting it from the command line. You can do this from Unix, DOS, or any other system, which provides you a command-line interpreter or shell window.

```
$perl  -e <perl code>       # Unix/Linux


or


C:>perl -e <perl code>      # Windows/DOS
```

Here is the list of all the available command line options −

Sr.No.	Option & Description
1	**-d[:debugger]** Runs program under debugger
2	**-Idirectory** Specifies @INC/#include directory
3	**-T** Enables tainting checks
4	**-t** Enables tainting warnings
5	**-U** Allows unsafe operations
6	**-w** Enables many useful warnings
7	**-W**

		Enables all warnings
8	**-X**	
		Disables all warnings
9	**-e program**	
		Runs Perl script sent in as program
10	**file**	
		Runs Perl script from a given file

Script from the Command-line

A Perl script is a text file, which keeps perl code in it and it can be executed at the command line by invoking the interpreter on your application, as in the following –

```
$perl  script.pl        # Unix/Linux
```

or

```
C:>perl script.pl       # Windows/DOS
```

Integrated Development Environment:

You can run Perl from a graphical user interface (GUI) environment as well. All you need is a GUI application on your system that supports Perl. You can download Padre, the Perl IDE. You can also use Eclipse Plugin EPIC - Perl Editor and IDE for Eclipse if you are familiar with Eclipse.

Before proceeding to the next chapter, make sure your environment is properly setup and working perfectly fine. If you are not able to setup the environment properly then you can take help from your system admininstrator.

All the examples given in subsequent chapters have been executed with v5.16.2 version available on the CentOS flavor of Linux.

Perl - Syntax Overview

Perl borrows syntax and concepts from many languages: awk, sed, C, Bourne Shell, Smalltalk, Lisp and even English. However, there are some definite differences between the languages. This chapter is designd to quickly get you up to speed on the syntax that is expected in Perl.

A Perl program consists of a sequence of declarations and statements, which run from the top to the bottom. Loops, subroutines, and other control structures allow you to jump around within the code. Every simple statement must end with a semicolon (;).

Perl is a free-form language: you can format and indent it however you like. Whitespace serves mostly to separate tokens, unlike languages like Python where it is an important part of the syntax, or Fortran where it is immaterial.

First Perl Program:

Interactive Mode Programming:

You can use Perl interpreter with -e option at command line, which lets you execute Perl statements from the command line. Let's try something at $ prompt as follows –

```
$perl -e 'print "Hello World\n"'
```

This execution will produce the following result –

Hello, world

Script Mode Programming

Assuming you are already on $ prompt, let's open a text file hello.pl using vi or vim editor and put the following lines inside your file.

```
#!/usr/bin/perl
```

```
# This will print "Hello, World"

print "Hello, world\n";
```

Here **/usr/bin/perl** is actual the perl interpreter binary. Before you execute your script, be sure to change the mode of the script file and give execution priviledge, generally a setting of 0755 works perfectly and finally you execute the above script as follows –

```
$chmod 0755 hello.pl
$./hello.pl
```

This execution will produce the following result –

Hello, world

You can use parentheses for functions arguments or omit them according to your personal taste. They are only required occasionally to clarify the issues of precedence. Following two statements produce the same result.

```perl
print("Hello, world\n");

print "Hello, world\n";
```

Perl File Extension:

A Perl script can be created inside of any normal simple-text editor program. There are several programs available for every type of platform. There are many programs designd for programmers available for download on the web.

As a Perl convention, a Perl file must be saved with a .pl or .PL file extension in order to be recognized as a functioning Perl script. File names can contain numbers, symbols, and letters but must not contain a space. Use an underscore (_) in places of spaces.

Comments in Perl:

Comments in any programming language are friends of developers. Comments can be used to make program user friendly and they are simply skipped by the interpreter without impacting the code functionality. For example, in the above program, a line starting with hash # is a comment.

Simply saying comments in Perl start with a hash symbol and run to the end of the line –

```
# This is a comment in perl
```

Lines starting with = are interpreted as the start of a section of embedded documentation (pod), and all subsequent lines until the next =cut are ignored by the compiler. Following is the example –

```
#!/usr/bin/perl


# This is a single line comment

print "Hello, world\n";


=begin comment

This is all part of multiline comment.

You can use as many lines as you like

These comments will be ignored by the

compiler until the next =cut is encountered.

=cut
```

This will produce the following result –

```
Hello, world
```

Whitespaces in Perl:

A Perl program does not care about whitespaces. Following program works perfectly fine −

```
#!/usr/bin/perl


print      "Hello, world\n";
```

But if spaces are inside the quoted strings, then they would be printed as is. For example −

```
#!/usr/bin/perl


# This would print with a line break in the middle
print "Hello

    world\n";
```

This will produce the following result −

```
Hello
    world
```

All types of whitespace like spaces, tabs, newlines, etc. are equivalent for the interpreter when they are used outside of the quotes. A line containing only whitespace, possibly with a comment, is known as a blank line, and Perl totally ignores it.

Single and Double Quotes in Perl:

You can use double quotes or single quotes around literal strings as follows –

```
#!/usr/bin/perl


print "Hello, world\n";

print 'Hello, world\n';
```

This will produce the following result –

```
Hello, world
Hello, world\n$
```

There is an important difference in single and double quotes. Only double quotes **interpolate** variables and special characters such as newlines \n, whereas single quote does not interpolate any variable or special character. Check below example where we are using $a as a variable to store a value and later printing that value –

```
#!/usr/bin/perl


$a = 10;

print "Value of a = $a\n";

print 'Value of a = $a\n';
```

This will produce the following result −

```
Value of a = 10
Value of a = $a\n$
```

"Here" Documents

You can store or print multiline text with a great comfort. Even you can make use of variables inside the "here" document. Below is a simple syntax, check carefully there must be no space between the << and the identifier.

An identifier may be either a bare word or some quoted text like we used EOF below. If identifier is quoted, the type of quote you use determines the treatment of the text inside the here docoment, just as in regular quoting. An unquoted identifier works like double quotes.

```
#!/usr/bin/perl


$a = 10;

$var = <<"EOF";

This is the syntax for here document and it will continue

until it encounters a EOF in the first line.

This is case of double quote so variable value will be

interpolated. For example value of a = $a
```

```
EOF

print "$var\n";
```

```
$var = <<'EOF';

This is case of single quote so variable value will be

interpolated. For example value of a = $a

EOF

print "$var\n";
```

This will produce the following result −

```
This is the syntax for here document and it will continue
until it encounters a EOF in the first line.
This is case of double quote so variable value will be
interpolated. For example value of a = 10

This is case of single quote so variable value will be
interpolated. For example value of a = $a
```

Escaping Characters

Perl uses the backslash (\) character to escape any type of character that might interfere with our code. Let's take one example where we want to print double quote and $ sign −

```
#!/usr/bin/perl
```

```
$result = "This is \"number\"";

print "$result\n";

print "\$result\n";
```

This will produce the following result −

```
This is "number"
$result
```

Perl Identifiers:

A Perl identifier is a name used to identify a variable, function, class, module, or other object. A Perl variable name starts with either $, @ or % followed by zero or more letters, underscores, and digits (0 to 9).

Perl does not allow punctuation characters such as @, $, and % within identifiers. Perl is a **case sensitive** programming language. Thus **$Manpower** and **$manpower** are two different identifiers in Perl.

Perl - Data Types

Perl is a loosely typed language and there is no need to specify a type for your data while using in your program. The Perl interpreter will choose the type based on the context of the data itself.

Perl has three basic data types: scalars, arrays of scalars, and hashes of scalars, also known as associative arrays. Here is a little detail about these data types.

Sr.No.	Types & Description
1	**Scalar** Scalars are simple variables. They are preceded by a dollar sign ($). A scalar is either a number, a string, or a reference. A reference is actually an address of a variable, which we will see in the upcoming chapters.
2	**Arrays** Arrays are ordered lists of scalars that you access with a numeric index, which starts with 0. They are preceded by an "at" sign (@).
3	**Hashes** Hashes are unordered sets of key/value pairs that

you access using the keys as subscripts. They are preceded by a percent sign (%).

Numeric Literals:

Perl stores all the numbers internally as either signed integers or double-precision floating-point values. Numeric literals are specified in any of the following floating-point or integer formats –

Type	Value
Integer	1234
Negative integer	-100
Floating point	2000
Scientific notation	16.12E14
Hexadecimal	0xffff
Octal	0577

String Literals:

Strings are sequences of characters. They are usually alphanumeric values delimited by either single (') or double (") quotes. They work much like UNIX shell quotes where you can use single quoted strings and double quoted strings.

Double-quoted string literals allow variable interpolation, and single-quoted strings are not. There are certain characters when they are proceeded by a back slash, have special meaning and they are used to represent like newline (\n) or tab (\t).

You can embed newlines or any of the following Escape sequences directly in your double quoted strings –

Escape sequence	Meaning
\\	Backslash
\'	Single quote
\"	Double quote

\a	Alert or bell
\b	Backspace
\f	Form feed
\n	Newline
\r	Carriage return
\t	Horizontal tab
\v	Vertical tab
\0nn	Creates Octal formatted numbers
\xnn	Creates Hexideciamal formatted numbers
\cX	Controls characters, x may be any character

\u	Forces next character to uppercase
\l	Forces next character to lowercase
\U	Forces all following characters to uppercase
\L	Forces all following characters to lowercase
\Q	Backslash all following non-alphanumeric characters
\E	End \U, \L, or \Q

Example:

Let's see again how strings behave with single quotation and double quotation. Here we will use string escapes mentioned in the above table and will make use of the scalar variable to assign string values.

```
#!/usr/bin/perl
```

```perl
# This is case of interpolation.

$str = "Welcome to \nPerl Tutorial!";

print "$str\n";


# This is case of non-interpolation.

$str = 'Welcome to \nPerl Tutorial!';

print "$str\n";


# Only W will become upper case.

$str = "\uwelcome to Perl Tutorial!";

print "$str\n";


# Whole line will become capital.

$str = "\UWelcome to Perl Tutorial!";

print "$str\n";


# A portion of line will become capital.

$str = "Welcome to \UPerl\Tutorial!";

print "$str\n";
```

```
# Backsalash non alpha-numeric including spaces.

$str = "\QWelcome to Perl's family";

print "$str\n";
```

This will produce the following result −

```
Welcome to
Perl Tutorial!
Welcome to \nPerl Tutorial!
Welcome to Perl Tutorial!
WELCOME TO PERL TUTORIAL!
Welcome to Perl Tutorial!
Welcome\ to\ Perl\'s\ family
```

Perl – Variables

Variables are the reserved memory locations to store values. This means that when you create a variable you reserve some space in memory.

Based on the data type of a variable, the interpreter allocates memory and decides what can be stored in the reserved memory. Therefore, by assigning different data types to variables, you can store integers, decimals, or strings in these variables.

We have learnt that Perl has the following three basic data types –

- Scalars
- Arrays
- Hashes

Accordingly, we are going to use three types of variables in Perl. A **scalar** variable will precede by a dollar sign ($) and it can store either a number, a string, or a reference. An **array** variable will precede by sign @ and it will store ordered lists of scalars. Finaly, the **Hash** variable will precede by sign % and will be used to store sets of key/value pairs.

Perl maintains every variable type in a separate namespace. So you can, without fear of conflict, use the same name for a scalar variable, an array, or a hash. This means that $foo and @foo are two different variables.

Creating Variables:

Perl variables do not have to be explicitly declared to reserve memory space. The declaration happens automatically when you assign a value to a variable. The equal sign (=) is used to assign values to variables.

Keep a note that this is mandatory to declare a variable before we use it if we use **use strict** statement in our program.

The operand to the left of the = operator is the name of the variable, and the operand to the right of the = operator is the value stored in the variable. For example −

```
$age = 25;          # An integer assignment

$name = "John Paul";   # A string

$salary = 1445.50;    # A floating point
```

Here 25, "John Paul" and 1445.50 are the values assigned to $age, $name and $salary variables,   respectively. Shortly we will see how we can assign values to arrays and hashes.

Scalar Variables:

A scalar is a single unit of data. That data might be an integer number, floating point, a character, a string, a paragraph, or an entire web page. Simply saying it could be anything, but only a single thing.

Here is a simple example of using scalar variables −

```perl
#!/usr/bin/perl


$age = 25;          # An integer assignment

$name = "John Paul";  # A string

$salary = 1445.50;    # A floating point


print "Age = $age\n";

print "Name = $name\n";

print "Salary = $salary\n";
```

This will produce the following result −

```
Age = 25
Name = John Paul
Salary = 1445.5
```

Array Variables:

An array is a variable that stores an ordered list of scalar values. Array variables are preceded by an "at" (@) sign. To refer to a single element of an array, you will use the dollar sign ($) with the variable name followed by the index of the element in square brackets.

Here is a simple example of using array variables −

```
#!/usr/bin/perl


@ages = (25, 30, 40);
@names = ("John Paul", "Lisa", "Kumar");


print "\$ages[0] = $ages[0]\n";
print "\$ages[1] = $ages[1]\n";
print "\$ages[2] = $ages[2]\n";
print "\$names[0] = $names[0]\n";
print "\$names[1] = $names[1]\n";
print "\$names[2] = $names[2]\n";
```

Here we used escape sign (\) before the $ sign just to print it. Other Perl will understand it as a variable and will print its value. When executed, this will produce the following result −

```
$ages[0] = 25
$ages[1] = 30
$ages[2] = 40
```

```
$names[0] = John Paul
$names[1] = Lisa
$names[2] = Kumar
```

Hash Variables:

A hash is a set of **key/value** pairs. Hash variables are preceded by a percent (%) sign. To refer to a single element of a hash, you will use the hash variable name followed by the "key" associated with the value in curly brackets.

Here is a simple example of using hash variables −

```
#!/usr/bin/perl


%data = ('John Paul', 45, 'Lisa', 30, 'Kumar', 40);


print "\$data{'John Paul'} = $data{'John Paul'}\n";

print "\$data{'Lisa'} = $data{'Lisa'}\n";

print "\$data{'Kumar'} = $data{'Kumar'}\n";
```

This will produce the following result −

```
$data{'John Paul'} = 45
$data{'Lisa'} = 30
$data{'Kumar'} = 40
```

Variable Context:

Perl treats same variable differently based on Context, i.e., situation where a variable is being used. Let's check the following example –

```perl
#!/usr/bin/perl

@names = ('John Paul', 'Lisa', 'Kumar');

@copy = @names;

$size = @names;

print "Given names are : @copy\n";

print "Number of names are : $size\n";
```

This will produce the following result –

```
Given names are : John Paul Lisa Kumar
Number of names are : 3
```

Here @names is an array, which has been used in two different contexts. First we copied it into anyother array, i.e., list, so it returned all the elements assuming that context is list context. Next we used the same array and tried to store this array in a scalar, so in this case it returned just the number of elements in this array assuming that context is scalar context. Following table lists down the various contexts –

Sr.No.	Context & Description
1	**Scalar** Assignment to a scalar variable evaluates the right-hand side in a scalar context.
2	**List** Assignment to an array or a hash evaluates the right-hand side in a list context.
3	**Boolean** Boolean context is simply any place where an expression is being evaluated to see whether it's true or false.
4	**Void** This context not only doesn't care what the return value is, it doesn't even want a return value.
5	**Interpolative** This context only happens inside quotes, or things that work like quotes.

Perl – Scalars

A scalar is a single unit of data. That data might be an integer number, floating point, a character, a string, a paragraph, or an entire web page.

Here is a simple example of using scalar variables –

```
#!/usr/bin/perl


$age = 25;          # An integer assignment
$name = "John Paul";   # A string
$salary = 1445.50;    # A floating point


print "Age = $age\n";
print "Name = $name\n";
print "Salary = $salary\n";
```

This will produce the following result –

```
Age = 25
Name = John Paul
Salary = 1445.5
```

Numeric Scalars:

A scalar is most often either a number or a string. Following example demonstrates the usage of various types of numeric scalars –

```perl
#!/usr/bin/perl

$integer = 200;

$negative = -300;

$floating = 200.340;

$bigfloat = -1.2E-23;


# 377 octal, same as 255 decimal

$octal = 0377;


# FF hex, also 255 decimal

$hexa = 0xff;


print "integer = $integer\n";

print "negative = $negative\n";
```

```perl
print "floating = $floating\n";

print "bigfloat = $bigfloat\n";

print "octal = $octal\n";

print "hexa = $hexa\n";
```

This will produce the following result −

```
integer = 200
negative = -300
floating = 200.34
bigfloat = -1.2e-23
octal = 255
hexa = 255
```

String Scalars:

Following example demonstrates the usage of various types of string scalars. Notice the difference between single quoted strings and double quoted strings −

```perl
#!/usr/bin/perl


$var = "This is string scalar!";

$quote = 'I m inside single quote - $var';

$double = "This is inside single quote - $var";
```

```
$escape = "This example of escape -\tHello, World!";
```

```
print "var = $var\n";

print "quote = $quote\n";

print "double = $double\n";

print "escape = $escape\n";
```

This will produce the following result −

```
var = This is string scalar!
quote = I m inside single quote - $var
double = This is inside single quote - This is string scalar!
escape = This example of escape -      Hello, World
```

Scalar Operations:

You will see a detail of various operators available in Perl in a separate chapter, but here we are going to list down few numeric and string operations.

```
#!/usr/bin/perl


$str = "hello" . "world";     # Concatenates strings.

$num = 5 + 10;                # adds two numbers.

$mul = 4 * 5;                 # multiplies two numbers.
```

```perl
$mix = $str . $num;          # concatenates string and
number.


print "str = $str\n";

print "num = $num\n";

print "mix = $mix\n";
```

This will produce the following result –

```
str = helloworld
num = 15
mul = 20
mix = helloworld15
```

Multiline Strings:

If you want to introduce multiline strings into your programs, you can use the standard single quotes as below –

```perl
#!/usr/bin/perl


$string = 'This is

a multiline

string';
```

```
print "$string\n";
```

This will produce the following result –

```
This is
a multiline
string
```

You can use "here" document syntax as well to store or print multilines as below –

```
#!/usr/bin/perl


print <<EOF;

This is

a multiline

string

EOF
```

This will also produce the same result –

```
This is
a multiline
string
```

V-Strings:

A literal of the form v1.20.300.4000 is parsed as a string composed of characters with the specified ordinals. This form is known as v-strings.

A v-string provides an alternative and more readable way to construct strings, rather than use the somewhat less readable interpolation form "\x{1}\x{14}\x{12c}\x{fa0}".

They are any literal that begins with a v and is followed by one or more dot-separated elements. For example –

```
#!/usr/bin/perl


$smile  = v9786;

$foo    = v102.111.111;

$martin = v77.97.114.116.105.110;


print "smile = $smile\n";

print "foo = $foo\n";

print "martin = $martin\n";
```

This will also produce the same result –

```
smile = ☺
foo = foo
```

martin = Martin
Wide character in print at main.pl line 7.

Special Literals:

So far you must have a feeling about string scalars and its concatenation and interpolation opration. So let me tell you about three special literals __FILE__, __LINE__, and __PACKAGE__ represent the current filename, line number, and package name at that point in your program.

They may be used only as separate tokens and will not be interpolated into strings. Check the below example –

```
#!/usr/bin/perl

print "File name ". __FILE__ . "\n";

print "Line Number " . __LINE__ ."\n";

print "Package " . __PACKAGE__ ."\n";

# they can not be interpolated

print "__FILE__ __LINE__ __PACKAGE__ \n";
```

This will produce the following result –

```
File name hello.pl
Line Number 4
Package main
__FILE__ __LINE__ __PACKAGE__
```

Perl – Arrays

An array is a variable that stores an ordered list of scalar values. Array variables are preceded by an "at" (@) sign. To refer to a single element of an array, you will use the dollar sign ($) with the variable name followed by the index of the element in square brackets.

Here is a simple example of using the array variables –

```
#!/usr/bin/perl


@ages = (25, 30, 40);

@names = ("John Paul", "Lisa", "Kumar");


print "\$ages[0] = $ages[0]\n";

print "\$ages[1] = $ages[1]\n";

print "\$ages[2] = $ages[2]\n";

print "\$names[0] = $names[0]\n";

print "\$names[1] = $names[1]\n";

print "\$names[2] = $names[2]\n";
```

Here we have used the escape sign (\) before the $ sign just to print it. Other Perl will understand it as a variable and will print its value. When executed, this will produce the following result –

```
$ages[0] = 25
$ages[1] = 30
$ages[2] = 40
$names[0] = John Paul
$names[1] = Lisa
$names[2] = Kumar
```

In Perl, List and Array terms are often used as if they're interchangeable. But the list is the data, and the array is the variable.

Array Creation:

Array variables are prefixed with the @ sign and are populated using either parentheses or the qw operator. For example −

```
@array = (1, 2, 'Hello');

@array = qw/This is an array/;
```

The second line uses the qw// operator, which returns a list of strings, separating the delimited string by white space. In this example, this leads to a four-element array; the first element is 'this' and last (fourth) is 'array'. This means that you can use different lines as follows −

```
@days = qw/Monday

Tuesday
```

```
...
Sunday/;
```

You can also populate an array by assigning each value individually as follows –

```
$array[0] = 'Monday';

...

$array[6] = 'Sunday';
```

Accessing Array Elements:

When accessing individual elements from an array, you must prefix the variable with a dollar sign ($) and then append the element index within the square brackets after the name of the variable. For example –

```
#!/usr/bin/perl


@days = qw/Mon Tue Wed Thu Fri Sat Sun/;


print "$days[0]\n";
print "$days[1]\n";
print "$days[2]\n";
```

```
print "$days[6]\n";

print "$days[-1]\n";

print "$days[-7]\n";
```

This will produce the following result –

```
Mon
Tue
Wed
Sun
Sun
Mon
```

Array indices start from zero, so to access the first element you need to give 0 as indices. You can also give a negative index, in which case you select the element from the end, rather than the beginning, of the array. This means the following –

```
print $days[-1]; # outputs Sun

print $days[-7]; # outputs Mon
```

Sequential Number Arrays:

Perl offers a shortcut for sequential numbers and letters. Rather than typing out each element when counting to 100 for example, we can do something like as follows –

```
#!/usr/bin/perl
```

```
@var_10 = (1..10);

@var_20 = (10..20);

@var_abc = (a..z);


print "@var_10\n";   # Prints number from 1 to 10

print "@var_20\n";   # Prints number from 10 to 20

print "@var_abc\n";  # Prints number from a to z
```

Here double dot (..) is called **range operator**. This will produce the following result –

```
1 2 3 4 5 6 7 8 9 10
10 11 12 13 14 15 16 17 18 19 20
a b c d e f g h i j k l m n o p q r s t u v w x y z
```

Array Size:

The size of an array can be determined using the scalar context on the array - the returned value will be the number of elements in the array –

```
@array = (1,2,3);

print "Size: ",scalar @array,"\n";
```

The value returned will always be the physical size of the array, not the number of valid elements. You can demonstrate this, and the difference between scalar @array and $#array, using this fragment is as follows −

```
#!/usr/bin/perl


@array = (1,2,3);

$array[50] = 4;


$size = @array;

$max_index = $#array;


print "Size: $size\n";

print "Max Index: $max_index\n";
```

This will produce the following result −

```
Size: 51
Max Index: 50
```

There are only four elements in the array that contains information, but the array is 51 elements long, with a highest index of 50.

Adding and Removing Elements in Array:

Perl provides a number of useful functions to add and remove elements in an array. You may have a question what is a function? So far you have used **print** function to print various values. Similarly there are various other functions or sometime called sub-routines, which can be used for various other functionalities.

Sr.No.	Types & Description
1	**push @ARRAY, LIST** Pushes the values of the list onto the end of the array.
2	**pop @ARRAY** Pops off and returns the last value of the array.
3	**shift @ARRAY** Shifts the first value of the array off and returns it, shortening the array by 1 and moving everything down.
4	**unshift @ARRAY, LIST** Prepends list to the front of the array, and returns

the number of elements in the new array.

```perl
#!/usr/bin/perl


# create a simple array
@coins = ("Quarter","Dime","Nickel");
print "1. \@coins = @coins\n";


# add one element at the end of the array
push(@coins, "Penny");
print "2. \@coins  = @coins\n";


# add one element at the beginning of the array
unshift(@coins, "Dollar");
print "3. \@coins  = @coins\n";


# remove one element from the last of the array.
pop(@coins);
print "4. \@coins  = @coins\n";
```

```
# remove one element from the beginning of the array.

shift(@coins);

print "5. \@coins  = @coins\n";
```

This will produce the following result –

```
1. @coins = Quarter Dime Nickel
2. @coins = Quarter Dime Nickel Penny
3. @coins = Dollar Quarter Dime Nickel Penny
4. @coins = Dollar Quarter Dime Nickel
5. @coins = Quarter Dime Nickel
```

Slicing Array Elements:

You can also extract a "slice" from an array - that is, you can select more than one item from an array in order to produce another array.

```
#!/usr/bin/perl


@days = qw/Mon Tue Wed Thu Fri Sat Sun/;


@weekdays = @days[3,4,5];
```

```
print "@weekdays\n";
```

This will produce the following result −

```
Thu Fri Sat
```

The specification for a slice must have a list of valid indices, either positive or negative, each separated by a comma. For speed, you can also use the .. range operator −

```
#!/usr/bin/perl

@days = qw/Mon Tue Wed Thu Fri Sat Sun/;

@weekdays = @days[3..5];

print "@weekdays\n";
```

This will produce the following result −

```
Thu Fri Sat
```

Replacing Array Elements

Now we are going to introduce one more function called **splice()**, which has the following syntax −

```
splice @ARRAY, OFFSET [ , LENGTH [ , LIST ] ]
```

This function will remove the elements of @ARRAY designated by OFFSET and LENGTH, and replaces them with LIST, if specified. Finally, it returns the elements removed from the array. Following is the example −

```
#!/usr/bin/perl

@nums = (1..20);
print "Before - @nums\n";


splice(@nums, 5, 5, 21..25);
print "After - @nums\n";
```

This will produce the following result −

```
Before - 1 2 3 4 5 6 7 8 9 10 11 12 13 14 15 16 17 18 19 20
After - 1 2 3 4 5 21 22 23 24 25 11 12 13 14 15 16 17 18 19
20
```

Here, the actual replacement begins with the 6th number after that five elements are then replaced from 6 to 10 with the numbers 21, 22, 23, 24 and 25.

Transform Strings to Arrays

Let's look into one more function called **split()**, which has the following syntax −

```
split [ PATTERN [ , EXPR [ , LIMIT ] ] ]
```

This function splits a string into an array of strings, and returns it. If LIMIT is specified, splits into at most that number of fields. If PATTERN is omitted, splits on whitespace. Following is the example −

```
#!/usr/bin/perl


# define Strings

$var_string = "Rain-Drops-On-Roses-And-Whiskers-On-Kittens";

$var_names = "Larry,David,Roger,Ken,Michael,Tom";


# transform above strings into arrays.

@string = split('-', $var_string);

@names = split(',', $var_names);
```

```perl
print "$string[3]\n"; # This will print Roses

print "$names[4]\n";  # This will print Michael
```

This will produce the following result −

```
Roses
Michael
```

Transform Arrays to Strings:

We can use the **join()** function to rejoin the array elements and form one long scalar string. This function has the following syntax −

```
join EXPR, LIST
```

This function joins the separate strings of LIST into a single string with fields separated by the value of EXPR, and returns the string. Following is the example −

```perl
#!/usr/bin/perl


# define Strings

$var_string = "Rain-Drops-On-Roses-And-Whiskers-On-Kittens";

$var_names = "Larry,David,Roger,Ken,Michael,Tom";
```

```
# transform above strings into arrays.

@string = split('-', $var_string);

@names  = split(',', $var_names);


$string1 = join( '-', @string );

$string2 = join( ',', @names );


print "$string1\n";

print "$string2\n";
```

This will produce the following result –

```
Rain-Drops-On-Roses-And-Whiskers-On-Kittens
Larry,David,Roger,Ken,Michael,Tom
```

Sorting Arrays:

The **sort()** function sorts each element of an array according to the ASCII Numeric standards. This function has the following syntax –

```
sort [ SUBROUTINE ] LIST
```

This function sorts the LIST and returns the sorted array value. If SUBROUTINE is specified then specified logic inside the SUBTROUTINE is applied while sorting the elements.

```
#!/usr/bin/perl


# define an array

@foods = qw(pizza steak chicken burgers);

print "Before: @foods\n";


# sort this array

@foods = sort(@foods);

print "After: @foods\n";
```

This will produce the following result −

```
Before: pizza steak chicken burgers
After: burgers chicken pizza steak
```

Please note that sorting is performed based on ASCII Numeric value of the words. So the best option is to first transform every element of the array into lowercase letters and then perform the sort function.

The $[Special Variable:

So far you have seen simple variable we defined in our programs and used them to store and print scalar and array values. Perl provides numerous special variables, which have their predefined meaning.

We have a special variable, which is written as **$[**. This special variable is a scalar containing the first index of all arrays. Because Perl arrays have zero-based indexing, $[will almost always be 0. But if you set $[to 1 then all your arrays will use on-based indexing. It is recommended not to use any other indexing other than zero. However, let's take one example to show the usage of $[variable −

```perl
#!/usr/bin/perl


# define an array

@foods = qw(pizza steak chicken burgers);

print "Foods: @foods\n";


# Let's reset first index of all the arrays.

$[ = 1;
```

```perl
print "Food at \@foods[1]: $foods[1]\n";

print "Food at \@foods[2]: $foods[2]\n";
```

This will produce the following result −

```
Foods: pizza steak chicken burgers
Food at @foods[1]: pizza
Food at @foods[2]: steak
```

Merging Arrays:

Because an array is just a comma-separated sequence of values, you can combine them together as shown below −

```perl
#!/usr/bin/perl


@numbers = (1,3,(4,5,6));


print "numbers = @numbers\n";
```

This will produce the following result −

```
numbers = 1 3 4 5 6
```

The embedded arrays just become a part of the main array as shown below −

```
#!/usr/bin/perl


@odd = (1,3,5);

@even = (2, 4, 6);


@numbers = (@odd, @even);


print "numbers = @numbers\n";
```

This will produce the following result –

```
numbers = 1 3 5 2 4 6
```

Selecting Elements from Lists:

The list notation is identical to that for arrays. You can extract an element from an array by appending square brackets to the list and giving one or more indices –

```
#!/usr/bin/perl


$var = (5,4,3,2,1)[4];


print "value of var = $var\n"
```

This will produce the following result –

value of var = 1

Similarly, we can extract slices, although without the requirement for a leading @ character –

```perl
#!/usr/bin/perl


@list = (5,4,3,2,1)[1..3];


print "Value of list = @list\n";
```

This will produce the following result –

Value of list = 4 3 2

Perl – Hashes

A hash is a set of **key/value** pairs. Hash variables are preceded by a percent (%) sign. To refer to a single element of a hash, you will use the hash variable name preceded by a "$" sign and followed by the "key" associated with the value in curly brackets..

Here is a simple example of using the hash variables –

```
#!/usr/bin/perl

%data = ('John Paul', 45, 'Lisa', 30, 'Kumar', 40);

print "\$data{'John Paul'} = $data{'John Paul'}\n";

print "\$data{'Lisa'} = $data{'Lisa'}\n";

print "\$data{'Kumar'} = $data{'Kumar'}\n";
```

This will produce the following result –

```
$data{'John Paul'} = 45
$data{'Lisa'} = 30
$data{'Kumar'} = 40
```

Creating Hashes:

Hashes are created in one of the two following ways. In the first method, you assign a value to a named key on a one-by-one basis −

```
$data{'John Paul'} = 45;

$data{'Lisa'} = 30;

$data{'Kumar'} = 40;
```

In the second case, you use a list, which is converted by taking individual pairs from the list: the first element of the pair is used as the key, and the second, as the value. For example −

```
%data = ('John Paul', 45, 'Lisa', 30, 'Kumar', 40);
```

For clarity, you can use => as an alias for , to indicate the key/value pairs as follows −

```
%data = ('John Paul' => 45, 'Lisa' => 30, 'Kumar' => 40);
```

Here is one more variant of the above form, have a look at it, here all the keys have been preceded by hyphen (-) and no quotation is required around them −

```
%data = (-JohnPaul => 45, -Lisa => 30, -Kumar => 40);
```

But it is important to note that there is a single word, i.e., without spaces keys have been used in this form of hash formation and if you build-up your hash this way then keys will be accessed using hyphen only as shown below.

```
$val = %data{-JohnPaul}

$val = %data{-Lisa}
```

Accessing Hash Elements:

When accessing individual elements from a hash, you must prefix the variable with a dollar sign ($) and then append the element key within curly brackets after the name of the variable. For example –

```
#!/usr/bin/perl
%data = ('John Paul' => 45, 'Lisa' => 30, 'Kumar' => 40);
print "$data{'John Paul'}\n";
print "$data{'Lisa'}\n";
print "$data{'Kumar'}\n";
```

This will produce the following result –

```
45
30
40
```

Extracting Slices:

You can extract slices of a hash just as you can extract slices from an array. You will need to use @ prefix for the variable to store the returned value because they will be a list of values −

```perl
#!/uer/bin/perl


%data = (-JohnPaul => 45, -Lisa => 30, -Kumar => 40);

@array = @data{-JohnPaul, -Lisa};

print "Array : @array\n";
```

This will produce the following result −

```
Array : 45 30
```

Extracting Keys and Values:

You can get a list of all of the keys from a hash by using **keys**function, which has the following syntax −

```perl
keys %HASH
```

This function returns an array of all the keys of the named hash. Following is the example −

```perl
#!/usr/bin/perl
```

```
%data = ('John Paul' => 45, 'Lisa' => 30, 'Kumar' => 40);
```

```
@names = keys %data;
```

```
print "$names[0]\n";
print "$names[1]\n";
print "$names[2]\n";
```

This will produce the following result −

```
Lisa
John Paul
Kumar
```

Similarly, you can use **values** function to get a list of all the values. This function has the following syntax −

```
values %HASH
```

This function returns a normal array consisting of all the values of the named hash. Following is the example −

```
#!/usr/bin/perl
```

```
%data = ('John Paul' => 45, 'Lisa' => 30, 'Kumar' => 40);
```

```
@ages = values %data;
```

```
print "$ages[0]\n";

print "$ages[1]\n";

print "$ages[2]\n";
```

This will produce the following result –

```
30
45
40
```

Checking for Existence:

If you try to access a key/value pair from a hash that doesn't exist, you'll normally get the **undefined** value, and if you have warnings switched on, then you'll get a warning generated at run time. You can get around this by using the **exists** function, which returns true if the named key exists, irrespective of what its value might be –

```
#!/usr/bin/perl

%data = ('John Paul' => 45, 'Lisa' => 30, 'Kumar' => 40);
```

```perl
if( exists($data{'Lisa'} ) ) {

    print "Lisa is $data{'Lisa'} years old\n";

} else {

    print "I don't know age of Lisa\n";

}
```

Here we have introduced the IF...ELSE statement, which we will study in a separate chapter. For now you just assume that **if(condition)** part will be executed only when the given condition is true otherwise **else** part will be executed. So when we execute the above program, it produces the following result because here the given condition *exists($data{'Lisa'}* returns true −

```
Lisa is 30 years old
```

Getting Hash Size:

You can get the size - that is, the number of elements from a hash by using the scalar context on either keys or values. Simply saying first you have to get an array of either the keys or values and then you can get the size of array as follows −

```perl
#!/usr/bin/perl
```

```
%data = ('John Paul' => 45, 'Lisa' => 30, 'Kumar' => 40);


@keys = keys %data;

$size = @keys;

print "1 - Hash size:  is $size\n";


@values = values %data;

$size = @values;

print "2 - Hash size:  is $size\n";
```

This will produce the following result −

```
1 - Hash size: is 3
2 - Hash size: is 3
```

Add and Remove Elements in Hashes:

Adding a new key/value pair can be done with one line of code using simple assignment operator. But to remove an element from the hash you need to use **delete** function as shown below in the example −

```
#!/usr/bin/perl
```

```perl
%data = ('John Paul' => 45, 'Lisa' => 30, 'Kumar' => 40);

@keys = keys %data;

$size = @keys;

print "1 - Hash size:  is $size\n";


# adding an element to the hash;

$data{'Ali'} = 55;

@keys = keys %data;

$size = @keys;

print "2 - Hash size:  is $size\n";


# delete the same element from the hash;

delete $data{'Ali'};

@keys = keys %data;

$size = @keys;

print "3 - Hash size:  is $size\n";
```

This will produce the following result −

```
1 - Hash size: is 3
2 - Hash size: is 4
3 - Hash size: is 3
```

Perl Conditional Statements - IF...ELSE

Perl conditional statements helps in the decision making, which require that the programmer specifies one or more conditions to be evaluated or tested by the program, along with a statement or statements to be executed if the condition is determined to be true, and optionally, other statements to be executed if the condition is determined to be false.

Following is the general from of a typical decision making structure found in most of the programming languages –

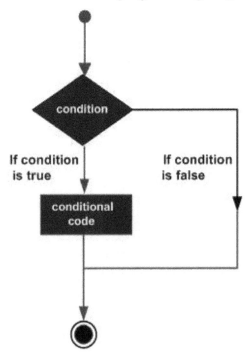

The number 0, the strings '0' and "" , the empty list () , and undef are all **false** in a boolean context and all other values are **true**. Negation of a true value by **!** or **not** returns a special false value.

Perl programming language provides the following types of conditional statements.

Sr.No.	Statement & Description
1	**if statement** An **if statement** consists of a boolean expression followed by one or more statements.
2	**if...else statement** An **if** **statement** can be followed by an optional **else statement**.
3	**if...elsif...else statement** An **if** **statement** can be followed by an optional **elsif** **statement** and then by an optional **else statement**.
4	**unless statement**

	An **unless statement** consists of a boolean expression followed by one or more statements.
5	**unless...else statement**
	An **unless statement** can be followed by an optional **else statement**.
6	**unless...elsif..else statement**
	An **unless statement** can be followed by an optional **elsif statement** and then by an optional **else statement**.
7	**switch statement**
	With the latest versions of Perl, you can make use of the **switch** statement. which allows a simple way of comparing a variable value against various conditions.

if statement:

A Perl **if** statement consists of a boolean expression followed by one or more statements. The if statement is same as in other programming languages. It is used to perform basic condition based task. It is used to decide whether a certain statement or block of statements will be executed or not i.e if a certain condition is true then a block of statement is executed otherwise not.

Syntax

The syntax of an **if** statement in Perl programming language is –

```
if(boolean_expression) {
   # statement(s) will execute if the given condition is true
}
```

If the boolean expression evaluates to **true** then the block of code inside the **if** statement will be executed. If boolean expression evaluates to **false** then the first set of code after the end of the **if** statement (after the closing curly brace) will be executed.

The number 0, the strings '0' and "" , the empty list () , and undef are all **false** in a boolean context and all other values are **true**. Negation of a true value by **!** or **not** returns a special false value.

Flow Diagram:

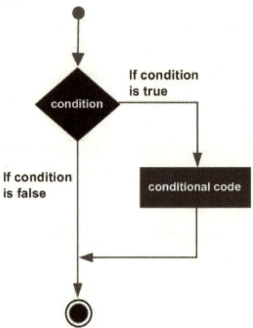

Example

```
#!/usr/local/bin/perl


$a = 10;

# check the boolean condition using if statement

if( $a < 20 ) {

   # if condition is true then print the following

   printf "a is less than 20\n";
```

```
}
```

print "value of a is : $a\n";

$a = "";

check the boolean condition using if statement

if($a) {

   # if condition is true then print the following

   printf "a has a true value\n";

```
}
```

print "value of a is : $a\n";

First IF statement makes use of less than operator (<), which compares two operands and if first operand is less than the second one then it returns true otherwise it returns false. So when the above code is executed, it produces the following result −

```
a is less than 20
value of a is : 10
value of a is :
```

if – else Statement:

A Perl **if** statement can be followed by an optional **else** statement, which executes when the boolean expression is false. The if statement evaluates the code if the condition is true but what if the condition is not true, here comes the else statement. It tells the code what to do when the if condition is false.

Syntax:

The syntax of an **if...else** statement in Perl programming language is −

```
if(boolean_expression) {
   # statement(s) will execute if the given condition is true
} else {
   # statement(s) will execute if the given condition is false
}
```

If the boolean expression evaluates to **true**, then the **if block** of code will be executed otherwise **else block** of code will be executed.

The number 0, the strings '0' and "" , the empty list () , and undef are all **false** in a boolean context and all other values are **true**. Negation of a true value by **!** or **not** returns a special false value.

Flow Diagram:

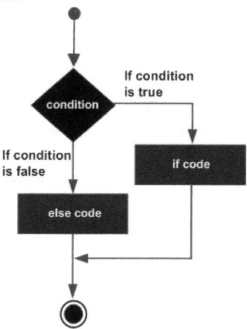

Example:

```
#!/usr/local/bin/perl


$a = 100;

# check the boolean condition using if statement

if( $a < 20 ) {

   # if condition is true then print the following

   printf "a is less than 20\n";
```

```perl
} else {
   # if condition is false then print the following
   printf "a is greater than 20\n";
}
print "value of a is : $a\n";


$a = "";
# check the boolean condition using if statement
if( $a ) {
   # if condition is true then print the following
   printf "a has a true value\n";
} else {
   # if condition is false then print the following
   printf "a has a false value\n";
}
print "value of a is : $a\n";
```

When the above code is executed, it produces the following result −

```
a is greater than 20
value of a is : 100
```

a has a false value
value of a is :

If – elsif – else ladder Statement:

An **if** statement can be followed by an optional **elsif...else** statement, which is very useful to test the various conditions using single if...elsif statement. Here, a user can decide among multiple options. The if statements are executed from the top down. As soon as one of the conditions controlling the if is true, the statement associated with that get executed, and the rest of the ladder is bypassed. If none of the conditions is true, then the final else statement will be executed.

When using **if** , **elsif** , **else** statements there are few points to keep in mind.

- An **if** can have zero or one **else**'s and it must come after any **elsif**'s.

- An **if** can have zero to many **elsif**'s and they must come before the **else**.

- Once an **elsif** succeeds, none of the remaining **elsif**'s or **else**'s will be tested.

Syntax:

The syntax of an **if...elsif...else** statement in Perl programming language is −

```
if(boolean_expression 1) {
   # Executes when the boolean expression 1 is true
} elsif( boolean_expression 2) {
   # Executes when the boolean expression 2 is true
} elsif( boolean_expression 3) {
   # Executes when the boolean expression 3 is true
} else {
   # Executes when the none of the above condition is true
}
```

Example:

```perl
#!/usr/local/bin/perl


$a = 100;

# check the boolean condition using if statement

if( $a == 20 ) {

   # if condition is true then print the following

   printf "a has a value which is 20\n";

} elsif( $a == 30 ) {

   # if condition is true then print the following

   printf "a has a value which is 30\n";

} else {

   # if none of the above conditions is true
```

```
printf "a has a value which is $a\n";

}
```

Here we are using the equality operator == which is used to check if two operands are equal or not. If both the operands are same, then it returns true otherwise it returns false. When the above code is executed, it produces the following result –

```
a has a value which is 100
```

unless Statement:

A Perl **unless** statement consists of a boolean expression followed by one or more statements. In this case if the condition is false then the statements will execute. The **number 0, the empty string "", charcter '0', the empty list (), and undef** are all **false** in a boolean context and all other values are true.

Syntax:

The syntax of an unless statement in Perl programming language is –

```
unless(boolean_expression) {
    # statement(s) will execute if the given condition is false
}
```

If the boolean expression evaluates to **false**, then the block of code inside the unless statement will be executed. If boolean expression evaluates to **true** then the first set of code after the end of the unless statement (after the closing curly brace) will be executed.

The number 0, the strings '0' and "" , the empty list () , and undef are all **false** in a boolean context and all other values are **true**. Negation of a true value by **!** or **not** returns a special false value.

Flow Diagram:

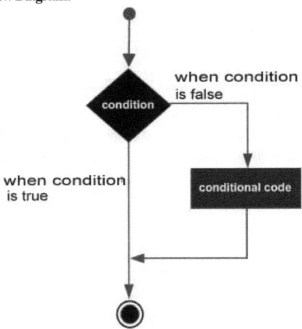

Example:

```perl
#!/usr/local/bin/perl



$a = 20;
# check the boolean condition using unless statement
unless( $a < 20 ) {
   # if condition is false then print the following
   printf "a is not less than 20\n";
}
print "value of a is : $a\n";


$a = "";
# check the boolean condition using unless statement
unless ( $a ) {
   # if condition is false then print the following
   printf "a has a false value\n";
}
print "value of a is : $a\n";
```

First unless statement makes use of less than operator (<), which compares two operands and if first operand is less than the second one then it returns true otherwise it returns false. So when the above code is executed, it produces the following result –

```
a is not less than 20
value of a is : 20
a has a false value
value of a is :
```

Unless-else Statement:

A Perl **unless** statement can be followed by an optional **else** statement, which executes when the boolean expression is true.

Syntax:

The syntax of an **unless...else** statement in Perl programming language is –

```
unless(boolean_expression) {
   # statement(s) will execute if the given condition is false
} else {
   # statement(s) will execute if the given condition is true
}
```

If the boolean expression evaluates to **true** then the **unless block** of code will be executed otherwise **else block** of code will be executed.

The number 0, the strings '0' and "" , the empty list () , and undef are all **false** in a boolean context and all other values are **true**. Negation of a true value by **!** or **not** returns a special false value.

Flow Diagram:

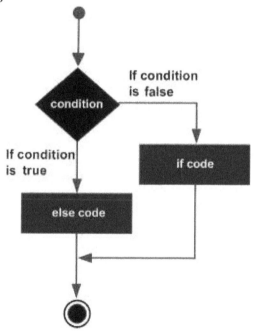

Example:

```perl
#!/usr/local/bin/perl


$a = 100;
# check the boolean condition using unless statement
unless( $a == 20 ) {
   # if condition is false then print the following
   printf "given condition is false\n";
} else {
   # if condition is true then print the following
   printf "given condition is true\n";
}
print "value of a is : $a\n";


$a = "";
# check the boolean condition using unless statement
unless( $a ) {
```

```
    # if condition is false then print the following

    printf "a has a false value\n";

} else {

    # if condition is true then print the following

    printf "a has a true value\n";

}

print "value of a is : $a\n";
```

When the above code is executed, it produces the following result −

```
given condition is false
value of a is : 100
a has a false value
value of a is :
```

Switch Statement:

A **switch** statement allows a variable to be tested for equality against a list of values. Each value is called a case, and the variable being switched on is checked for each **switch case**.

A switch case implementation is dependent on **Switch** module and **Switch** module has been implemented using *Filter::Util::Call* and *Text::Balanced* and requires both these modules to be installed.

Syntax:

The synopsis for a **switch** statement in Perl programming language is as follows −

```
use Switch;

switch(argument) {
    case 1          { print "number 1" }
    case "a"        { print "string a" }
    case [1..10,42] { print "number in list" }
    case (\@array)  { print "number in list" }
    case /\w+/      { print "pattern" }
    case qr/\w+/    { print "pattern" }
    case (\%hash)   { print "entry in hash" }
    case (\&sub)    { print "arg to subroutine" }
    else            { print "previous case not true" }
}
```

The following rules apply to a **switch** statement −

- The **switch** statement takes a single scalar argument of any type, specified in parentheses.

- The value is followed by a block, which may contain one or more case statement followed by a block of Perl statement(s).

- A case statement takes a single scalar argument and selects the appropriate type of matching between the case argument and the current switch value.

- If the match is successful, the mandatory block associated with the case statement is executed.

- A **switch** statement can have an optional **else** case, which must appear at the end of the switch. The default case can be used for performing a task when none of the cases is matched.

- If a case block executes an untargeted **next**, control is immediately transferred to the statement after the case statement (i.e., usually another case), rather than out of the surrounding switch block.

- Not every case needs to contain a **next**. If no **next**appears, the flow of control will *not fall through*subsequent cases.

Flow Diagram:

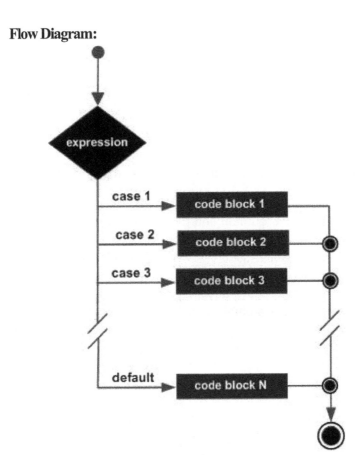

Example:

```
#!/usr/local/bin/perl


use Switch;
```

```
$var = 10;

@array = (10, 20, 30);

%hash = ('key1' => 10, 'key2' => 20);


switch($var) {

    case 10         { print "number 100\n" }

    case "a"        { print "string a" }

    case [1..10,42]  { print "number in list" }

    case (\@array)   { print "number in list" }

    case (\%hash)    { print "entry in hash" }

    else            { print "previous case not true" }

}
```

When the above code is executed, it produces the following result −

```
number 100
```

Fall-though is usually a bad idea in a switch statement. However, now consider a fall-through case, we will use the **next** to transfer the control to the next matching case, which is a list in this case −

```
#!/usr/local/bin/perl
```

```
use Switch;

$var = 10;

@array = (10, 20, 30);

%hash = ('key1' => 10, 'key2' => 20);


switch($var) {

    case 10          { print "number 100\n"; next; }

    case "a"         { print "string a" }

    case [1..10,42]   { print "number in list" }

    case (\@array)    { print "number in list" }

    case (\%hash)     { print "entry in hash" }

    else             { print "previous case not true" }

}
```

When the above code is executed, it produces the following result –

```
number 100
number in list
```

The ? : Operator

Let's check the **conditional operator ? :**which can be used to replace **if...else** statements. It has the following general form −

```
Exp1 ? Exp2 : Exp3;
```

Where Exp1, Exp2, and Exp3 are expressions. Notice the use and placement of the colon.

The value of a ? expression is determined like this: Exp1 is evaluated. If it is true, then Exp2 is evaluated and becomes the value of the entire ? expression. If Exp1 is false, then Exp3 is evaluated and its value becomes the value of the expression. Below is a simple example making use of this operator −

```
#!/usr/local/bin/perl

$name = "Ali";

$age = 10;

$status = ($age > 60 )? "A senior citizen" : "Not a senior citizen";

print "$name is  - $status\n";
```

This will produce the following result −

```
Ali is - Not a senior citizen
```

Perl – Loops

There may be a situation when you need to execute a block of code several number of times. In general, statements are executed sequentially: The first statement in a function is executed first, followed by the second, and so on.

Programming languages provide various control structures that allow for more complicated execution paths.

A loop statement allows us to execute a statement or group of statements multiple times and following is the general form of a loop statement in most of the programming languages –

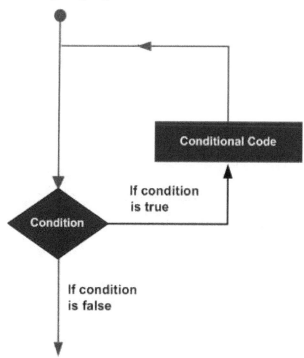

Perl programming language provides the following types of loop to handle the looping requirements.

Sr.No.	Loop Type & Description
1	**while loop** Repeats a statement or group of statements while a given condition is true. It tests the condition before executing the loop body.
2	**until loop** Repeats a statement or group of statements until a given condition becomes true. It tests the condition before executing the loop body.
3	**for loop** Executes a sequence of statements multiple times and abbreviates the code that manages the loop variable.
4	**foreach loop** The foreach loop iterates over a normal list value

and sets the variable VAR to be each element of the list in turn.

| 5 | **do...while loop** |
| | Like a while statement, except that it tests the condition at the end of the loop body |

| 6 | **nested loops** |
| | You can use one or more loop inside any another while, for or do..while loop. |

For Loop:

A **for** loop is a repetition control structure that allows you to efficiently write a loop that needs to execute a specific number of times. **"for" loop** provides a concise way of writing the loop structure. Unlike a while loop, a for statement consumes the initialization, condition and increment/decrement in one line thereby providing a shorter, easy to debug structure of looping.

Syntax

The syntax of a **for** loop in Perl programming language is –

```
for ( init; condition; increment ) {
   statement(s);
}
```

Here is the flow of control in a **for** loop –

- The **init** step is executed first, and only once. This step allows you to declare and initialize any loop control variables. You are not required to put a statement here, as long as a semicolon appears.

- Next, the **condition** is evaluated. If it is true, the body of the loop is executed. If it is false, the body of the loop does not execute and flow of control jumps to the next statement just after the for loop.

- After the body of the for loop executes, the flow of control jumps back up to the **increment** statement. This statement allows you to update any loop control variables. This statement can be left blank, as long as a semicolon appears after the condition.

- The condition is now evaluated again. If it is true, the loop executes and the process repeats itself (body of loop, then increment step, and then again condition). After the condition becomes false, the for loop terminates.

Flow Diagram

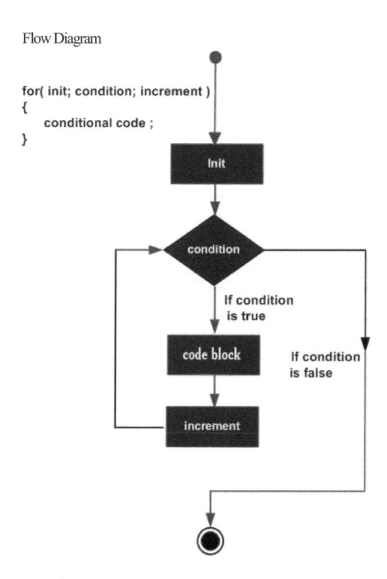

```perl
for( init; condition; increment )
{
    conditional code ;
}
```

Example

Live Demo

```perl
#!/usr/local/bin/perl
```

```
# for loop execution

for( $a = 10; $a < 20; $a = $a + 1 ) {

   print "value of a: $a\n";

}
```

When the above code is executed, it produces the following result −

```
value of a: 10
value of a: 11
value of a: 12
value of a: 13
value of a: 14
value of a: 15
value of a: 16
value of a: 17
value of a: 18
value of a: 19
```

While Loop:

A **while** loop statement in Perl programming language repeatedly executes a target statement as long as a given condition is true. A while loop generally takes an expression in parenthesis. If the expression is True then the code within the body of while loop is executed. A while loop is used when we don't know the number of times we want the loop to be executed however we know the termination condition of the loop. It is also known as a **entry controlled loop** as the condition is checked before executing the loop. The while loop can be thought of as a repeating if statement.

Syntax:

The syntax of a **while** loop in Perl programming language is –

```
while(condition) {
   statement(s);
}
```

Here **statement(s)** may be a single statement or a block of statements. The **condition** may be any expression. The loop iterates while the condition is true. When the condition becomes false, program control passes to the line immediately following the loop.

The number 0, the strings '0' and "" , the empty list () , and undef are all **false** in a boolean context and all other values are **true**. Negation of a true value by **!** or **not** returns a special false value.

Flow Diagram:

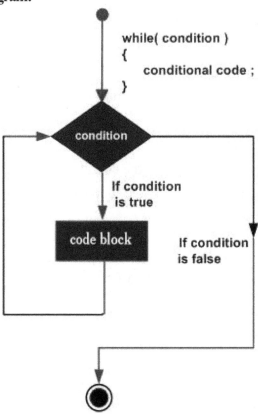

Here the key point of the *while* loop is that the loop might not ever run. When the condition is tested and the result is false, the loop body will be skipped and the first statement after the while loop will be executed.

Example:

```perl
#!/usr/local/bin/perl


$a = 10;


# while loop execution
while( $a < 20 ) {
   printf "Value of a: $a\n";
    $a = $a + 1;
}
```

Here we are using the comparison operator < to compare value of variable $a against 20. So while value of $a is less than 20, **while** loop continues executing a block of code next to it and as soon as the value of $a becomes equal to 20, it comes out. When executed, above code produces the following result −

```
Value of a: 10
Value of a: 11
Value of a: 12
Value of a: 13
```

```
Value of a: 14
Value of a: 15
Value of a: 16
Value of a: 17
Value of a: 18
Value of a: 19
```

Until loop:

An **until** loop statement in Perl programming language repeatedly executes a target statement as long as a given condition is false.

Syntax:

The syntax of an **until** loop in Perl programming language is –

```
until(condition) {
   statement(s);
}
```

Here **statement(s)** may be a single statement or a block of statements. The **condition** may be any expression. The loop iterates until the condition becomes true. When the condition becomes true, the program control passes to the line immediately following the loop.

The number 0, the strings '0' and "" , the empty list () , and undef are all **false** in a boolean context and all other values are **true**. Negation of a true value by **!** or **not** returns a special false value.

Flow Diagram:

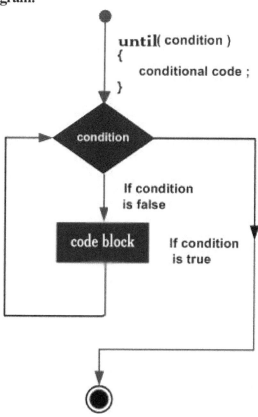

Here key point of the *until* loop is that the loop might not ever run. When the condition is tested and the result is true, the loop body will be skipped and the first statement after the until loop will be executed.

Example:

```perl
#!/usr/local/bin/perl


$a = 5;


# until loop execution
until( $a > 10 ) {
   printf "Value of a: $a\n";
    $a = $a + 1;
}
```

Here we are using the comparison operator > to compare value of variable $a against 10. So until the value of $a is less than 10, **until** loop continues executing a block of code next to it and as soon as the value of $a becomes greater than 10, it comes out. When executed, above code produces the following result –

```
Value of a: 5
Value of a: 6
Value of a: 7
Value of a: 8
Value of a: 9
Value of a: 10
```

Foreach Loop:

The **foreach** loop iterates over a list value and sets the control variable (var) to be each element of the list in turn –

Syntax:

The syntax of a **foreach** loop in Perl programming language is –

```
foreach var (list) {
...
}
```

Flow Diagram:

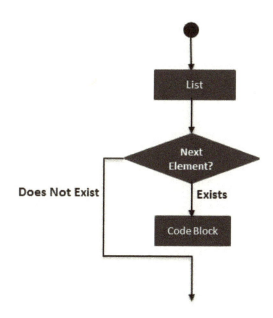

Example:

```perl
#!/usr/local/bin/perl


@list = (2, 20, 30, 40, 50);


# foreach loop execution
foreach $a (@list) {
   print "value of a: $a\n";
}
```

When the above code is executed, it produces the following result −

```
value of a: 2
value of a: 20
value of a: 30
value of a: 40
value of a: 50
```

do...while Loop:

Unlike **for** and **while** loops, which test the loop condition at the top of the loop, the **do...while** loop checks its condition at the bottom of the loop.

A do..while loop is almost same as a while loop. The only difference is that do..while loop runs at least one time. The condition is checked after the first execution. A do..while loop is used when we want the loop to run at least one time. It is also known as **exit controlled loop** as the condition is checked after executing the loop.

Syntax:

The syntax of a **do...while** loop in Perl is −

```
do {
   statement(s);
}while( condition );
```

It should be noted that the conditional expression appears at the end of the loop, so the statement(s) in the loop executes once before the condition is tested. If the condition is true, the flow of control jumps back up to do, and the statement(s) in the loop executes again. This process repeats until the given condition becomes false.

The number 0, the strings '0' and "" , the empty list () , and undef are all **false** in a boolean context and all other values are **true**. Negation of a true value by ! or **not** returns a special false value.

Flow Diagram:

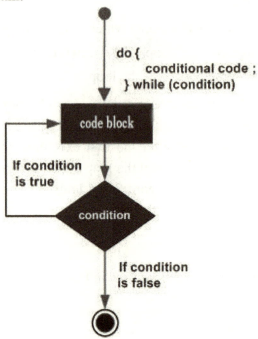

Example:

```perl
#!/usr/local/bin/perl


$a = 10;


# do...while loop execution

do {

    printf "Value of a: $a\n";
```

```
    $a = $a + 1;

}while( $a < 20 );
```

When the above code is executed, it produces the following result −

```
Value of a: 10
Value of a: 11
Value of a: 12
Value of a: 13
Value of a: 14
Value of a: 15
Value of a: 16
Value of a: 17
Value of a: 18
Value of a: 19
```

Loop Control Statements:

Loop control statements change the execution from its normal sequence. When execution leaves a scope, all automatic objects that were created in that scope are destroyed.

Perl supports the following control statements. Click the following links to check their detail.

Sr.No.	Control Statement & Description
1	**next statement** Causes the loop to skip the remainder of its body and immediately retest its condition prior to reiterating.
2	**last statement** Terminates the loop statement and transfers execution to the statement immediately following the loop.
3	**continue statement** A continue BLOCK, it is always executed just before the conditional is about to be evaluated

again.

| 4 | **redo statement** |

The redo command restarts the loop block without evaluating the conditional again. The continue block, if any, is not executed.

| 5 | **goto statement** |

Perl supports a goto command with three forms: goto label, goto expr, and goto &name.

The Infinite Loop:

A loop becomes infinite loop if a condition never becomes false. The **for** loop is traditionally used for this purpose. Since none of the three expressions that form the **for** loop are required, you can make an endless loop by leaving the conditional expression empty.

```perl
#!/usr/local/bin/perl

for( ; ; ) {
   printf "This loop will run forever.\n";
}
```

You can terminate the above infinite loop by pressing the Ctrl + C keys.

When the conditional expression is absent, it is assumed to be true. You may have an initialization and increment expression, but as a programmer more commonly use the for (;;) construct to signify an infinite loop.

Perl – Operators

What is an Operator?

Simple answer can be given using the expression *4 + 5 is equal to 9*. Here 4 and 5 are called operands and + is called operator. Perl language supports many operator types, but following is a list of important and most frequently used operators –

- Arithmetic Operators
- Equality Operators
- Logical Operators
- Assignment Operators
- Bitwise Operators
- Logical Operators
- Quote-like Operators
- Miscellaneous Operators

Lets have a look at all the operators one by one.

Perl Arithmetic Operators:

Assume variable $a holds 10 and variable $b holds 20, then following are the Perl arithmatic operators −

Sr.No.	Operator & Description
1	**+ (Addition)** Adds values on either side of the operator **Example** − $a + $b will give 30
2	**- (Subtraction)** Subtracts right hand operand from left hand operand **Example** − $a - $b will give -10
3	*** (Multiplication)** Multiplies values on either side of the operator **Example** − $a * $b will give 200
4	**/ (Division)** Divides left hand operand by right hand operand **Example** − $b / $a will give 2

5	**% (Modulus)**
	Divides left hand operand by right hand operand and returns remainder
	Example − $b % $a will give 0
6	**** (Exponent)**
	Performs exponential (power) calculation on operators
	Example − $a**$b will give 10 to the power 20

Example:

Try the following example to understand all the arithmatic operators available in Perl. Copy and paste the following Perl program in test.pl file and execute this program.

```perl
#!/usr/local/bin/perl


$a = 21;

$b = 10;


print "Value of \$a = $a and value of \$b = $b\n";
```

```perl
$c = $a + $b;

print 'Value of $a + $b = ' . $c . "\n";


$c = $a - $b;

print 'Value of $a - $b = ' . $c . "\n";


$c = $a * $b;

print 'Value of $a * $b = ' . $c . "\n";


$c = $a / $b;

print 'Value of $a / $b = ' . $c . "\n";


$c = $a % $b;

print 'Value of $a % $b = ' . $c. "\n";


$a = 2;

$b = 4;

$c = $a ** $b;
```

```
print 'Value of $a ** $b = ' . $c . "\n";
```

When the above code is executed, it produces the following result –

```
Value of $a = 21 and value of $b = 10

Value of $a + $b = 31

Value of $a - $b = 11

Value of $a * $b = 210

Value of $a / $b = 2.1

Value of $a % $b = 1

Value of $a ** $b = 16
```

Perl Equality Operators:

These are also called relational operators. Assume variable $a holds 10 and variable $b holds 20 then, lets check the following numeric equality operators –

Sr.No.	Operator & Description
1	**== (equal to)** Checks if the value of two operands are equal or not, if yes then condition becomes true. **Example** – ($a == $b) is not true.
2	**!= (not equal to)** Checks if the value of two operands are equal or not, if values are not equal then condition becomes true. **Example** – ($a != $b) is true.
3	**<=>** Checks if the value of two operands are equal or not, and returns -1, 0, or 1 depending on whether the left argument is numerically less than, equal

	to, or greater than the right argument. **Example** − ($a <=> $b) returns -1.
4	**> (greater than)** Checks if the value of left operand is greater than the value of right operand, if yes then condition becomes true. **Example** − ($a > $b) is not true.
5	**< (less than)** Checks if the value of left operand is less than the value of right operand, if yes then condition becomes true. **Example** − ($a < $b) is true.
6	**>= (greater than or equal to)** Checks if the value of left operand is greater than or equal to the value of right operand, if yes then condition becomes true. **Example** − ($a >= $b) is not true.
7	**<= (less than or equal to)**

Checks if the value of left operand is less than or equal to the value of right operand, if yes then condition becomes true.

Example – ($a <= $b) is true.

Example:

Try the following example to understand all the numeric equality operators available in Perl. Copy and paste the following Perl program in test.pl file and execute this program.

```perl
#!/usr/local/bin/perl

$a = 21;
$b = 10;

print "Value of \$a = $a and value of \$b = $b\n";

if( $a == $b ) {
   print "$a == \$b is true\n";
} else {
```

```perl
   print "\$a == \$b is not true\n";
}


if( $a != $b ) {

   print "\$a != \$b is true\n";
} else {

   print "\$a != \$b is not true\n";

}


$c = $a <=> $b;

print "\$a <=> \$b returns $c\n";


if( $a > $b ) {

   print "\$a > \$b is true\n";
} else {

   print "\$a > \$b is not true\n";

}

if( $a >= $b ) {
```

```perl
    print "\$a >= \$b is true\n";
} else {
    print "\$a >= \$b is not true\n";
}


if( $a < $b ) {
    print "\$a < \$b is true\n";
} else {
    print "\$a < \$b is not true\n";
}


if( $a <= $b ) {
    print "\$a <= \$b is true\n";
} else {
    print "\$a <= \$b is not true\n";
}
```

When the above code is executed, it produces the following result −

```
Value of $a = 21 and value of $b = 10
$a == $b is not true
```

```
$a != $b is true
$a <=> $b returns 1
$a > $b is true
$a >= $b is true
$a < $b is not true
$a <= $b is not true
```

Below is a list of equity operators. Assume variable $a holds "abc" and variable $b holds "xyz" then, lets check the following string equality operators −

Sr.No.	Operator & Description
1	**lt** Returns true if the left argument is stringwise less than the right argument. **Example** − ($a lt $b) is true.
2	**gt** Returns true if the left argument is stringwise greater than the right argument. **Example** − ($a gt $b) is false.

3	**le**
	Returns true if the left argument is stringwise less than or equal to the right argument.
	Example − ($a le $b) is true.
4	**ge**
	Returns true if the left argument is stringwise greater than or equal to the right argument.
	Example − ($a ge $b) is false.
5	**eq**
	Returns true if the left argument is stringwise equal to the right argument.
	Example − ($a eq $b) is false.
6	**ne**
	Returns true if the left argument is stringwise not equal to the right argument.
	Example − ($a ne $b) is true.
7	**cmp**
	Returns -1, 0, or 1 depending on whether the left

argument is stringwise less than, equal to, or greater than the right argument.

Example − ($a cmp $b) is -1.

Example

Try the following example to understand all the string equality operators available in Perl. Copy and paste the following Perl program in test.pl file and execute this program.

```perl
#!/usr/local/bin/perl


$a = "abc";

$b = "xyz";



print "Value of \$a = $a and value of \$b = $b\n";


if( $a lt $b ) {

   print "$a lt \$b is true\n";

} else {

   print "\$a lt \$b is not true\n";
```

```perl
}


if( $a gt $b ) {

   print "\$a gt \$b is true\n";

} else {

   print "\$a gt \$b is not true\n";

}


if( $a le $b ) {

   print "\$a le \$b is true\n";

} else {

   print "\$a le \$b is not true\n";

}


if( $a ge $b ) {

   print "\$a ge \$b is true\n";

} else {

   print "\$a ge \$b is not true\n";

}
```

```perl
if( $a ne $b ) {

   print "\$a ne \$b is true\n";

} else {

   print "\$a ne \$b is not true\n";

}


$c = $a cmp $b;

print "\$a cmp \$b returns $c\n";
```

When the above code is executed, it produces the following result −

```
Value of $a = abc and value of $b = xyz
abc lt $b is true
$a gt $b is not true
$a le $b is true
$a ge $b is not true
$a ne $b is true
$a cmp $b returns -1
```

Perl Assignment Operators:

Assume variable $a holds 10 and variable $b holds 20, then below are the assignment operators available in Perl and their usage −

Sr.No.	Operator & Description
1	= Simple assignment operator, Assigns values from right side operands to left side operand **Example** − $c = $a + $b will assigned value of $a + $b into $c
2	+= Add AND assignment operator, It adds right operand to the left operand and assign the result to left operand **Example** − $c += $a is equivalent to $c = $c + $a

3	-=
	Subtract AND assignment operator, It subtracts right operand from the left operand and assign the result to left operand
	Example – $c -= $a is equivalent to $c = $c - $a
4	*=
	Multiply AND assignment operator, It multiplies right operand with the left operand and assign the result to left operand
	Example – $c *= $a is equivalent to $c = $c * $a
5	/=
	Divide AND assignment operator, It divides left operand with the right operand and assign the result to left operand
	Example – $c /= $a is equivalent to $c = $c / $a
6	%=
	Modulus AND assignment operator, It takes modulus using two operands and assign the result to left operand

	Example – $c %= $a is equivalent to $c = $c % a
7	**=
	Exponent AND assignment operator, Performs exponential (power) calculation on operators and assign value to the left operand
	Example – $c **= $a is equivalent to $c = $c ** $a

Example:

Try the following example to understand all the assignment operators available in Perl. Copy and paste the following Perl program in test.pl file and execute this program.

```perl
#!/usr/local/bin/perl

$a = 10;
$b = 20;

print "Value of \$a = $a and value of \$b = $b\n";
```

```perl
$c = $a + $b;

print "After assignment value of \$c = $c\n";


$c += $a;

print "Value of \$c = $c after statement \$c += \$a\n";


$c -= $a;

print "Value of \$c = $c after statement \$c -= \$a\n";


$c *= $a;

print "Value of \$c = $c after statement \$c *= \$a\n";


$c /= $a;

print "Value of \$c = $c after statement \$c /= \$a\n";


$c %= $a;

print "Value of \$c = $c after statement \$c %= \$a\n";
```

```
$c = 2;

$a = 4;

print "Value of \$a = $a and value of \$c = $c\n";

$c **= $a;

print "Value of \$c = $c after statement \$c **= \$a\n";
```

When the above code is executed, it produces the following result –

```
Value of $a = 10 and value of $b = 20
After assignment value of $c = 30
Value of $c = 40 after statement $c += $a
Value of $c = 30 after statement $c -= $a
Value of $c = 300 after statement $c *= $a
Value of $c = 30 after statement $c /= $a
Value of $c = 0 after statement $c %= $a
Value of $a = 4 and value of $c = 2
Value of $c = 16 after statement $c **= $a
```

Perl Bitwise Operators:

Bitwise operator works on bits and perform bit by bit operation. Assume if $a = 60; and $b = 13; Now in binary format they will be as follows −

$a = 0011 1100

$b = 0000 1101

$a&$b = 0000 1100

$a|$b = 0011 1101

$a^$b = 0011 0001

~$a = 1100 0011

There are following Bitwise operators supported by Perl language, assume if $a = 60; and $b = 13

Sr.No.	Operator & Description
1	**&** Binary AND Operator copies a bit to the result if it exists in both operands. **Example** − ($a & $b) will give 12 which is 0000

	1100	
2	|	Binary OR Operator copies a bit if it exists in eather operand.

Example − ($a \| $b) will give 61 which is 0011 1101 |
| 3 | ^ | Binary XOR Operator copies the bit if it is set in one operand but not both.

Example − ($a ^ $b) will give 49 which is 0011 0001 |
| 4 | ~ | Binary Ones Complement Operator is unary and has the efect of 'flipping' bits.

Example − (~$a) will give -61 which is 1100 0011 in 2's complement form due to a signed binary number. |
| 5 | << | Binary Left Shift Operator. The left operands |

	value is moved left by the number of bits specified by the right operand. **Example** – $a << 2 will give 240 which is 1111 0000
6	>> Binary Right Shift Operator. The left operands value is moved right by the number of bits specified by the right operand. **Example** – $a >> 2 will give 15 which is 0000 1111

Example:

Try the following example to understand all the bitwise operators available in Perl. Copy and paste the following Perl program in test.pl file and execute this program.

```
#!/usr/local/bin/perl

use integer;

$a = 60;
```

```perl
$b = 13;


print "Value of \$a = $a and value of \$b = $b\n";


$c = $a & $b;
print "Value of \$a & \$b = $c\n";


$c = $a | $b;
print "Value of \$a | \$b = $c\n";


$c = $a ^ $b;
print "Value of \$a ^ \$b = $c\n";


$c = ~$a;
print "Value of ~\$a = $c\n";


$c = $a << 2;
print "Value of \$a << 2 = $c\n";
```

```
$c = $a >> 2;

print "Value of \$a >> 2 = $c\n";
```

When the above code is executed, it produces the following result –

```
Value of $a = 60 and value of $b = 13
Value of $a & $b = 12
Value of $a | $b = 61
Value of $a ^ $b = 49
Value of ~$a = -61
Value of $a << 2 = 240
Value of $a >> 2 = 15
```

Perl Logical Operators:

There are following logical operators supported by Perl language. Assume variable $a holds true and variable $b holds false then −

Sr.No.	Operator & Description
1	**and** Called Logical AND operator. If both the operands are true then then condition becomes true. **Example** − ($a and $b) is false.
2	**&&** C-style Logical AND operator copies a bit to the result if it exists in both operands. **Example** − ($a && $b) is false.
3	**or** Called Logical OR Operator. If any of the two operands are non zero then then condition becomes true.

	Example − ($a or $b) is true.
4	**||** C-style Logical OR operator copies a bit if it exists in eather operand. **Example** − ($a || $b) is true.
5	**not** Called Logical NOT Operator. Use to reverses the logical state of its operand. If a condition is true then Logical NOT operator will make false. **Example** − not($a and $b) is true.

Example

Try the following example to understand all the logical operators available in Perl. Copy and paste the following Perl program in test.pl file and execute this program.

```perl
#!/usr/local/bin/perl


$a = true;

$b = false;
```

```perl
print "Value of \$a = $a and value of \$b = $b\n";


$c = ($a and $b);
print "Value of \$a and \$b = $c\n";


$c = ($a  && $b);
print "Value of \$a && \$b = $c\n";


$c = ($a or $b);
print "Value of \$a or \$b = $c\n";


$c = ($a || $b);
print "Value of \$a || \$b = $c\n";


$a = 0;
$c = not($a);
print "Value of not(\$a)= $c\n";
```

When the above code is executed, it produces the following result –

```
Value of $a = true and value of $b = false
Value of $a and $b = false
Value of $a && $b = false
Value of $a or $b = true
Value of $a || $b = true
Value of not($a)= 1
```

Quote-like Operators:

There are following Quote-like operators supported by Perl language. In the following table, a {} represents any pair of delimiters you choose.

Sr.No.	Operator & Description
1	**q{ }** Encloses a string with-in single quotes **Example** – q{abcd} gives 'abcd'
2	**qq{ }** Encloses a string with-in double quotes **Example** – qq{abcd} gives "abcd"
3	**qx{ }** Encloses a string with-in invert quotes **Example** – qx{abcd} gives `abcd`

Example:

Try the following example to understand all the quote-like operators available in Perl. Copy and paste the following Perl program in test.pl file and execute this program.

```
#!/usr/local/bin/perl


$a = 10;


$b = q{a = $a};
print "Value of q{a = \$a} = $b\n";


$b = qq{a = $a};
print "Value of qq{a = \$a} = $b\n";


# unix command execution
$t = qx{date};
print "Value of qx{date} = $t\n";
```

When the above code is executed, it produces the following result −

```
Value of q{a = $a} = a = $a
```

Value of qq{a = $a} = a = 10
Value of qx{date} = Thu Feb 14 08:13:17 MST 2013

Miscellaneous Operators:

There are following miscellaneous operators supported by Perl language. Assume variable a holds 10 and variable b holds 20 then −

Sr.No.	Operator & Description
1	**.** Binary operator dot (.) concatenates two strings. **Example** − If $a = "abc", $b = "def" then $a.$b will give "abcdef"
2	**x** The repetition operator x returns a string consisting of the left operand repeated the number of times specified by the right operand. **Example** − ('-' x 3) will give ---.
3	**..**

	The range operator .. returns a list of values counting (up by ones) from the left value to the right value **Example** − (2..5) will give (2, 3, 4, 5)
4	**++** Auto Increment operator increases integer value by one **Example** − $a++ will give 11
5	**--** Auto Decrement operator decreases integer value by one **Example** − $a-- will give 9
6	**->** The arrow operator is mostly used in dereferencing a method or variable from an object or a class name **Example** − $obj->$a is an example to access variable $a from object $obj.

Example:

Try the following example to understand all the miscellaneous operators available in Perl. Copy and paste the following Perl program in test.pl file and execute this program.

```perl
#!/usr/local/bin/perl

$a = "abc";
$b = "def";

print "Value of \$a  = $a and value of \$b = $b\n";

$c = $a . $b;
print "Value of \$a . \$b = $c\n";

$c = "-" x 3;
print "Value of \"-\" x 3 = $c\n";

@c = (2..5);
```

```perl
print "Value of (2..5) = @c\n";


$a = 10;

$b = 15;

print "Value of \$a  = $a and value of \$b = $b\n";


$a++;

$c = $a ;

print "Value of \$a after \$a++ = $c\n";


$b--;

$c = $b ;

print "Value of \$b after \$b-- = $c\n";
```

When the above code is executed, it produces the following result −

```
Value of $a = abc and value of $b = def
Value of $a . $b = abcdef
Value of "-" x 3 = ---
Value of (2..5) = 2 3 4 5
Value of $a = 10 and value of $b = 15
Value of $a after $a++ = 11
Value of $b after $b-- = 14
```

We will explain --> operator when we will discuss about Perl Object and Classes.

Perl Operators Precedence:

The following table lists all operators from highest precedence to lowest.

```
left        terms and list operators (leftward)
left        ->
nonassoc ++ --
right       **
right       ! ~ \ and unary + and -
left        =~ !~
left        * / % x
left        + - .
left        << >>
nonassoc named unary operators
nonassoc < > <= >= lt gt le ge
nonassoc == != <=> eq ne cmp ~~
left        &
left        | ^
left        &&
left        || //
nonassoc .. ...
right       ?:
right       = += -= *= etc.
left        , =>
nonassoc list operators (rightward)
right       not
left        and
left        or xor
```

Example:

Try the following example to understand all the perl operators precedence in Perl. Copy and paste the following Perl program in test.pl file and execute this program.

```perl
#!/usr/local/bin/perl


$a = 20;

$b = 10;

$c = 15;

$d = 5;

$e;


print "Value of \$a  = $a, \$b = $b, \$c = $c and \$d = $d\n";


$e = ($a + $b) * $c / $d;

print "Value of (\$a + \$b) * \$c / \$d is  = $e\n";


$e = (($a + $b) * $c )/ $d;
```

```
print "Value of ((\$a + \$b) * \$c) / \$d is  = $e\n";



$e = ($a + $b) * ($c / $d);

print "Value of (\$a + \$b) * (\$c / \$d ) is  = $e\n";



$e = $a + ($b * $c ) / $d;

print "Value of \$a + (\$b * \$c )/ \$d is  = $e\n";
```

When the above code is executed, it produces the following result −

```
Value of $a = 20, $b = 10, $c = 15 and $d = 5
Value of ($a + $b) * $c / $d is = 90
Value of (($a + $b) * $c) / $d is = 90
Value of ($a + $b) * ($c / $d ) is = 90
Value of $a + ($b * $c )/ $d is = 50
```

Perl - Date and Time

This chapter will give you the basic understanding on how to process and manipulate dates and times in Perl.

Current Date and Time:

Let's start with **localtime()** function, which returns values for the current date and time if given no arguments. Following is the 9-element list returned by the **localtime** function while using in list context −

```
sec,    # seconds of minutes from 0 to 61
min,    # minutes of hour from 0 to 59
hour,   # hours of day from 0 to 24
mday,   # day of month from 1 to 31
mon,    # month of year from 0 to 11
year,   # year since 1900
wday,   # days since sunday
yday,   # days since January 1st
isdst   # hours of daylight savings time
```

Try the following example to print different elements returned by localtime() function −

```
#!/usr/local/bin/perl


@months = qw( Jan Feb Mar Apr May Jun Jul Aug Sep
Oct Nov Dec );

@days = qw(Sun Mon Tue Wed Thu Fri Sat Sun);
```

```
($sec,$min,$hour,$mday,$mon,$year,$wday,$yday,$isdst)
= localtime();

print "$mday $months[$mon] $days[$wday]\n";
```

When the above code is executed, it produces the following result −

```
16 Feb Sat
```

If you will use localtime() function in scalar context, then it will return date and time from the current time zone set in the system. Try the following example to print current date and time in full format −

```
#!/usr/local/bin/perl


$datestring = localtime();

print "Local date and time $datestring\n";
```

When the above code is executed, it produces the following result −

```
Local date and time Sat Feb 16 06:50:45 2013
```

GMT Time:

The function **gmtime()** works just like localtime() function but the returned values are localized for the standard Greenwich time zone. When called in list context, $isdst, the last value returned by gmtime, is always 0. There is no Daylight Saving Time in GMT.

You should make a note on the fact that localtime() will return the current local time on the machine that runs the script and gmtime() will return the universal Greenwich Mean Time, or GMT (or UTC).

Try the following example to print the current date and time but on GMT scale −

```perl
#!/usr/local/bin/perl


$datestring = gmtime();

print "GMT date and time $datestring\n";
```

When the above code is executed, it produces the following result −

```
GMT date and time Sat Feb 16 13:50:45 2013
```

Format Date and Time:

You can use localtime() function to get a list of 9-elements and later you can use the **printf()** function to format date and time based on your requirements as follows −

```perl
#!/usr/local/bin/perl
```

```perl
($sec,$min,$hour,$mday,$mon,$year,$wday,$yday,$isdst)
= localtime();
```

```perl
printf("Time Format - HH:MM:SS\n");
```

```perl
printf("%02d:%02d:%02d", $hour, $min, $sec);
```

When the above code is executed, it produces the following result −

```
Time Format - HH:MM:SS
06:58:52
```

Epoch time:

You can use the time() function to get epoch time, i.e., the numbers of seconds that have elapsed since a given date, in Unix is January 1, 1970.

```perl
#!/usr/local/bin/perl
```

```perl
$epoc = time();
```

```perl
print "Number of seconds since Jan 1, 1970 - $epoc\n";
```

When the above code is executed, it produces the following result −

Number of seconds since Jan 1, 1970 - 1361022130

You can convert a given number of seconds into date and time string as follows −

```perl
#!/usr/local/bin/perl


$datestring = localtime();

print "Current date and time $datestring\n";


$epoc = time();

$epoc = $epoc - 24 * 60 * 60;   # one day before of current date.


$datestring = localtime($epoc);

print "Yesterday's date and time $datestring\n";
```

When the above code is executed, it produces the following result −

Current date and time Tue Jun 5 05:54:43 2018
Yesterday's date and time Mon Jun 4 05:54:43 2018

POSIX Function strftime():

You can use the POSIX function **strftime()** to format date and time with the help of the following table. Please note that the specifiers marked with an asterisk (*) are locale-dependent.

Specifier	Replaced by	Example
%a	Abbreviated weekday name *	Thu
%A	Full weekday name *	Thursday
%b	Abbreviated month name *	Aug
%B	Full month name *	August
%c	Date and time representation *	Thu Aug 23 14:55:02 2001
%C	Year divided by 100 and truncated to integer (00-99)	20

%d	Day of the month, zero-padded (01-31)	23
%D	Short MM/DD/YY date, equivalent to %m/%d/%y	08/23/01
%e	Day of the month, space-padded (1-31)	23
%F	Short YYYY-MM-DD date, equivalent to %Y-%m-%d	2001-08-23
%g	Week-based year, last two digits (00-99)	01
%G	Week-based year	2001
%h	Abbreviated month name * (same as %b)	Aug
%H	Hour in 24h format (00-23)	14
%I	Hour in 12h format (01-12)	02

%j	Day of the year (001-366)	235
%m	Month as a decimal number (01-12)	08
%M	Minute (00-59)	55
%n	New-line character ('\n')	
%p	AM or PM designation	PM
%r	12-hour clock time *	02:55:02 pm
%R	24-hour HH:MM time, equivalent to %H:%M	14:55
%S	Second (00-61)	02
%t	Horizontal-tab character ('\t')	
%T	ISO 8601 time format (HH:MM:SS), equivalent	14:55

	to %H:%M:%S	
%u	ISO 8601 weekday as number with Monday as 1 (1-7)	4
%U	Week number with the first Sunday as the first day of week one (00-53)	33
%V	ISO 8601 week number (00-53)	34
%w	Weekday as a decimal number with Sunday as 0 (0-6)	4
%W	Week number with the first Monday as the first day of week one (00-53)	34
%x	Date representation *	08/23/01
%X	Time representation *	14:55:02
%y	Year, last two digits (00-99)	01

%Y	Year	2001
%z	ISO 8601 offset from UTC in timezone (1 minute = 1, 1 hour = 100)\n\nIf timezone cannot be termined, no characters	+100
%Z	Timezone name or abbreviation *\n\nIf timezone cannot be termined, no characters	CDT
%%	A % sign	%

Let's check the following example to understand the usage –

```
#!/usr/local/bin/perl

use POSIX qw(strftime);


$datestring = strftime "%a %b %e %H:%M:%S %Y",
localtime;
```

```perl
printf("date and time - $datestring\n");
```

```perl
# or for GMT formatted appropriately for your locale:

$datestring = strftime "%a %b %e %H:%M:%S %Y", gmtime;

printf("date and time - $datestring\n");
```

When the above code is executed, it produces the following result –

```
date and time - Sat Feb 16 07:10:23 2013
date and time - Sat Feb 16 14:10:23 2013
```

Perl – Subroutines

A Perl subroutine or function is a group of statements that together performs a task. You can divide up your code into separate subroutines. How you divide up your code among different subroutines is up to you, but logically the division usually is so each function performs a specific task.

Perl uses the terms subroutine, method and function interchangeably.

Define and Call a Subroutine:

The general form of a subroutine definition in Perl programming language is as follows –

```
sub subroutine_name {
   body of the subroutine
}
```

The typical way of calling that Perl subroutine is as follows –

```
subroutine_name( list of arguments );
```

In versions of Perl before 5.0, the syntax for calling subroutines was slightly different as shown below. This still works in the newest versions of Perl, but it is not recommended since it bypasses the subroutine prototypes.

```
&subroutine_name( list of arguments );
```

Let's have a look into the following example, which defines a simple function and then call it. Because Perl compiles your program before executing it, it doesn't matter where you declare your subroutine.

```perl
#!/usr/bin/perl


# Function definition

sub Hello {

   print "Hello, World!\n";

}


# Function call

Hello();
```

When above program is executed, it produces the following result –

```
Hello, World!
```

Passing Arguments to a Subroutine:

You can pass various arguments to a subroutine like you do in any other programming language and they can be acessed inside the function using the special array @_. Thus the first argument to the function is in $_[0], the second is in $_[1], and so on.

You can pass arrays and hashes as arguments like any scalar but passing more than one array or hash normally causes them to lose their separate identities. So we will use references (explained in the next chapter) to pass any array or hash.

Let's try the following example, which takes a list of numbers and then prints their average –

```perl
#!/usr/bin/perl


# Function definition
sub Average {
    # get total number of arguments passed.
    $n = scalar(@_);
    $sum = 0;


    foreach $item (@_) {
        $sum += $item;
    }
    $average = $sum / $n;
```

```
    print "Average for the given numbers : $average\n";

}
```

```
# Function call

Average(10, 20, 30);
```

When above program is executed, it produces the following result −

```
Average for the given numbers : 20
```

Passing Lists to Subroutines:

Because the @_ variable is an array, it can be used to supply lists to a subroutine. However, because of the way in which Perl accepts and parses lists and arrays, it can be difficult to extract the individual elements from @_. If you have to pass a list along with other scalar arguments, then make list as the last argument as shown below −

```
#!/usr/bin/perl

# Function definition

sub PrintList {

    my @list = @_;
```

```perl
   print "Given list is @list\n";
}

$a = 10;

@b = (1, 2, 3, 4);


# Function call with list parameter

PrintList($a, @b);
```

When above program is executed, it produces the following result –

```
Given list is 10 1 2 3 4
```

Passing Hashes to Subroutines:

When you supply a hash to a subroutine or operator that accepts a list, then hash is automatically translated into a list of key/value pairs. For example –

```perl
#!/usr/bin/perl


# Function definition

sub PrintHash {

  my (%hash) = @_;
```

```perl
   foreach my $key ( keys %hash ) {

     my $value = $hash{$key};

     print "$key : $value\n";

   }

}

%hash = ('name' => 'Tom', 'age' => 19);


# Function call with hash parameter

PrintHash(%hash);
```

When above program is executed, it produces the following result –

```
name : Tom
age : 19
```

Returning Value from a Subroutine:

You can return a value from subroutine like you do in any other programming language. If you are not returning a value from a subroutine then whatever calculation is last performed in a subroutine is automatically also the return value.

You can return arrays and hashes from the subroutine like any scalar but returning more than one array or hash normally causes them to lose their separate identities. So we will use references (explained in the next chapter) to return any array or hash from a function.

Let's try the following example, which takes a list of numbers and then returns their average −

```perl
#!/usr/bin/perl


# Function definition
sub Average {
    # get total number of arguments passed.
    $n = scalar(@_);
    $sum = 0;


    foreach $item (@_) {
        $sum += $item;
    }
    $average = $sum / $n;
```

```
   return $average;

}


# Function call

$num = Average(10, 20, 30);

print "Average for the given numbers : $num\n";
```

When above program is executed, it produces the following result −

Average for the given numbers : 20

Private Variables in a Subroutine:

By default, all variables in Perl are global variables, which means they can be accessed from anywhere in the program. But you can create **private** variables called **lexical variables** at any time with the **my** operator.

The **my** operator confines a variable to a particular region of code in which it can be used and accessed. Outside that region, this variable cannot be used or accessed. This region is called its scope. A lexical scope is usually a block of code with a set of braces around it, such as those defining the body of the subroutine or those marking the code blocks of *if, while, for, foreach,* and *eval* statements.

Following is an example showing you how to define a single or multiple private variables using **my** operator −

```perl
sub somefunc {

   my $variable; # $variable is invisible outside somefunc()

   my ($another, @an_array, %a_hash); # declaring many
variables at once

}
```

Let's check the following example to distinguish between global and private variables −

```perl
#!/usr/bin/perl


# Global variable

$string = "Hello, World!";


# Function definition

sub PrintHello {

   # Private variable for PrintHello function

   my $string;

   $string = "Hello, Perl!";

   print "Inside the function $string\n";
```

```
}

# Function call

PrintHello();

print "Outside the function $string\n";
```

When above program is executed, it produces the following result −

```
Inside the function Hello, Perl!
Outside the function Hello, World!
```

Temporary Values via local():

The **local** is mostly used when the current value of a variable must be visible to called subroutines. A local just gives temporary values to global (meaning package) variables. This is known as *dynamic scoping*. Lexical scoping is done with my, which works more like C's auto declarations.

If more than one variable or expression is given to local, they must be placed in parentheses. This operator works by saving the current values of those variables in its argument list on a hidden stack and restoring them upon exiting the block, subroutine, or eval.

Let's check the following example to distinguish between global and local variables –

```perl
#!/usr/bin/perl


# Global variable

$string = "Hello, World!";


sub PrintHello {

    # Private variable for PrintHello function

    local $string;

    $string = "Hello, Perl!";

    PrintMe();

    print "Inside the function PrintHello $string\n";

}
sub PrintMe {

    print "Inside the function PrintMe $string\n";

}


# Function call
```

```
PrintHello();

print "Outside the function $string\n";
```

When above program is executed, it produces the following result −

```
Inside the function PrintMe Hello, Perl!
Inside the function PrintHello Hello, Perl!
Outside the function Hello, World!
```

State Variables via state():

There are another type of lexical variables, which are similar to private variables but they maintain their state and they do not get reinitialized upon multiple calls of the subroutines. These variables are defined using the **state** operator and available starting from Perl 5.9.4.

Let's check the following example to demonstrate the use of **state** variables −

```perl
#!/usr/bin/perl

use feature 'state';

sub PrintCount {
  state $count = 0; # initial value
```

```perl
    print "Value of counter is $count\n";

    $count++;

}


for (1..5) {

    PrintCount();

}
```

When above program is executed, it produces the following result −

```
Value of counter is 0
Value of counter is 1
Value of counter is 2
Value of counter is 3
Value of counter is 4
```

Prior to Perl 5.10, you would have to write it like this −

```perl
#!/usr/bin/perl


{

    my $count = 0; # initial value
```

```perl
sub PrintCount {

  print "Value of counter is $count\n";

  $count++;

 }

}


for (1..5) {

  PrintCount();

}
```

Subroutine Call Context:

The context of a subroutine or statement is defined as the type of return value that is expected. This allows you to use a single function that returns different values based on what the user is expecting to receive. For example, the following localtime() returns a string when it is called in scalar context, but it returns a list when it is called in list context.

```perl
my $datestring = localtime( time );
```

In this example, the value of $timestr is now a string made up of the current date and time, for example, Thu Nov 30 15:21:33 2000. Conversely –

```
($sec,$min,$hour,$mday,$mon, $year,$wday,$yday,$isdst)
= localtime(time);
```

Now the individual variables contain the corresponding values returned by localtime() subroutine.

Perl – References

A Perl reference is a scalar data type that holds the location of another value which could be scalar, arrays, or hashes. Because of its scalar nature, a reference can be used anywhere, a scalar can be used.

You can construct lists containing references to other lists, which can contain references to hashes, and so on. This is how the nested data structures are built in Perl.

Create References

It is easy to create a reference for any variable, subroutine or value by prefixing it with a backslash as follows –

```
$scalarref = \$foo;
$arrayref  = \@ARGV;
$hashref   = \%ENV;
$coderef   = \&handler;
$globref   = \*foo;
```

You cannot create a reference on an I/O handle (filehandle or dirhandle) using the backslash operator but a reference to an anonymous array can be created using the square brackets as follows –

```
$arrayref = [1, 2, ['a', 'b', 'c']];
```

Similar way you can create a reference to an anonymous hash using the curly brackets as follows –

```
$hashref = {
```

```
'Adam' => 'Eve',

'Clyde' => 'Bonnie',

};
```

A reference to an anonymous subroutine can be created by using sub without a subname as follows −

```
$coderef = sub { print "Boink!\n" };
```

Dereferencing:

Dereferencing returns the value from a reference point to the location. To dereference a reference simply use $, @ or % as prefix of the reference variable depending on whether the reference is pointing to a scalar, array, or hash. Following is the example to explain the concept −

```
#!/usr/bin/perl


$var = 10;


# Now $r has reference to $var scalar.

$r = \$var;
```

```
# Print value available at the location stored in $r.

print "Value of $var is : ", $$r, "\n";


@var = (1, 2, 3);

# Now $r has reference to @var array.

$r = \@var;

# Print values available at the location stored in $r.

print "Value of @var is : ",  @$r, "\n";


%var = ('key1' => 10, 'key2' => 20);

# Now $r has reference to %var hash.

$r = \%var;

# Print values available at the location stored in $r.

print "Value of %var is : ", %$r, "\n";
```

When above program is executed, it produces the following result −

```
Value of 10 is : 10
Value of 1 2 3 is : 123
Value of %var is : key220key110
```

If you are not sure about a variable type, then its easy to know its type using **ref**, which returns one of the following strings if its argument is a reference. Otherwise, it returns false –

```
SCALAR
ARRAY
HASH
CODE
GLOB
REF
```

Let's try the following example –

```perl
#!/usr/bin/perl


$var = 10;

$r = \$var;

print "Reference type in r : ", ref($r), "\n";


@var = (1, 2, 3);

$r = \@var;

print "Reference type in r : ", ref($r), "\n";


%var = ('key1' => 10, 'key2' => 20);

$r = \%var;

print "Reference type in r : ", ref($r), "\n";
```

When above program is executed, it produces the following result –

```
Reference type in r : SCALAR
Reference type in r : ARRAY
Reference type in r : HASH
```

Circular References:

A circular reference occurs when two references contain a reference to each other. You have to be careful while creating references otherwise a circular reference can lead to memory leaks. Following is an example –

```perl
#!/usr/bin/perl

my $foo = 100;
$foo = \$foo;

print "Value of foo is : ", $$foo, "\n";
```

When above program is executed, it produces the following result –

```
Value of foo is : REF(0x9aae38)
```

References to Functions:

This might happen if you need to create a signal handler so you can produce a reference to a function by preceding that function name with \& and to dereference that reference you simply need to prefix reference variable using ampersand &. Following is an example –

```perl
#!/usr/bin/perl


# Function definition
sub PrintHash {
  my (%hash) = @_;


  foreach $item (%hash) {
    print "Item : $item\n";
  }
}
%hash = ('name' => 'Tom', 'age' => 19);


# Create a reference to above function.
$cref = \&PrintHash;
```

```
# Function call using reference.

&$cref(%hash);
```

When above program is executed, it produces the following result –

```
Item : name
Item : Tom
Item : age
Item : 19
```

Perl – Formats

Perl uses a writing template called a 'format' to output reports. To use the format feature of Perl, you have to define a format first and then you can use that format to write formatted data.

Define a Format:

Following is the syntax to define a Perl format –

```
format FormatName =

fieldline

value_one, value_two, value_three

fieldline

value_one, value_two

.
```

Here **FormatName** represents the name of the format. The **fieldline** is the specific way, the data should be formatted. The values lines represent the values that will be entered into the field line. You end the format with a single period.

Next **fieldline** can contain any text or fieldholders. The fieldholders hold space for data that will be placed there at a later date. A fieldholder has the format –

```
@<<<<
```

This fieldholder is left-justified, with a field space of 5. You must count the @ sign and the < signs to know the number of spaces in the field. Other field holders include –

@>>>> right-justified

@|||| centered

@####.## numeric field holder

@* multiline field holder

An example format would be –

format EMPLOYEE =

===

@<<<<<<<<<<<<<<<<<<<<<<< @<<

$name $age

@#####.##

$salary

===

In this example, $name would be written as left justify within 22 character spaces and after that age will be written in two spaces.

Using the Format"

In order to invoke this format declaration, we would use the **write** keyword –

```
write EMPLOYEE;
```

The problem is that the format name is usually the name of an open file handle, and the write statement will send the output to this file handle. As we want the data sent to the STDOUT, we must associate EMPLOYEE with the STDOUT filehandle. First, however, we must make sure that that STDOUT is our selected file handle, using the select() function.

```
select(STDOUT);
```

We would then associate EMPLOYEE with STDOUT by setting the new format name with STDOUT, using the special variable $~ or $FORMAT_NAME as follows –

```
$~ = "EMPLOYEE";
```

When we now do a write(), the data would be sent to STDOUT. Remember: if you are going to write your report in any other file handle instead of STDOUT then you can use select() function to select that file handle and rest of the logic will remain the same.

Let's take the following example. Here we have hard coded values just for showing the usage. In actual usage you will read values from a file or database to generate actual reports and you may need to write final report again into a file.

```perl
#!/usr/bin/perl


format EMPLOYEE =
========================================
@<<<<<<<<<<<<<<<<<<<<<<<<<< @<<
$name $age
@#####.##
$salary
========================================

.



select(STDOUT);
$~ = EMPLOYEE;


@n = ("Ali", "Raza", "Jaffer");
```

```perl
@a = (20,30, 40);
@s = (2000.00, 2500.00, 4000.000);


$i = 0;
foreach (@n) {
  $name = $_;
  $age = $a[$i];
  $salary = $s[$i++];
  write;
}
```

When executed, this will produce the following result −

```
==========================================
Ali              20
  2000.00
==========================================

==========================================
Raza             30
  2500.00
==========================================

==========================================
Jaffer           40
  4000.00
==========================================
```

Define a Report Header:

Everything looks fine. But you would be interested in adding a header to your report. This header will be printed on top of each page. It is very simple to do this. Apart from defining a template you would have to define a header and assign it to $^ or $FORMAT_TOP_NAME variable –

```perl
#!/usr/bin/perl


format EMPLOYEE =

===================================================

@<<<<<<<<<<<<<<<<<<<<<<<<<<< @<<
$name $age
@#####.##
$salary

===================================================

.


format EMPLOYEE_TOP =
===================================================
Name            Age
```

```
=================================================


select(STDOUT);

$~ = EMPLOYEE;

$^ = EMPLOYEE_TOP;


@n = ("Ali", "Raza", "Jaffer");

@a  = (20,30, 40);

@s = (2000.00, 2500.00, 4000.000);


$i = 0;

foreach (@n) {

  $name = $_;

  $age = $a[$i];

  $salary = $s[$i++];

  write;

}
```

Now your report will look like −

```
====================================================
Name              Age
====================================================

====================================================
Ali               20
  2000.00
====================================================

====================================================
Raza              30
  2500.00
====================================================

====================================================
Jaffer            40
  4000.00
====================================================
```

Define a Pagination:

What about if your report is taking more than one page? You have a solution for that, simply use **$%** or $FORMAT_PAGE_NUMBER vairable along with header as follows −

```
format EMPLOYEE_TOP =
====================================================
Name              Age Page @<
                          $%
====================================================
.
```

Now your output will look like as follows −

```
====================================================
```

```
Name            Age Page 1
==========================================
==========================================
Ali             20
 2000.00
------------------------------------------
------------------------------------------
Raza            30
 2500.00
------------------------------------------
------------------------------------------
Jaffer          40
 4000.00
------------------------------------------
```

Number of Lines on a Page:

You can set the number of lines per page using special variable $= (or $FORMAT_LINES_PER_PAGE), By default $= will be 60.

Define a Report Footer:

While $^ or $FORMAT_TOP_NAME contains the name of the current header format, there is no corresponding mechanism to automatically do the same thing for a footer. If you have a fixed-size footer, you can get footers by checking variable $- or $FORMAT_LINES_LEFT before each write() and print the footer yourself if necessary using another format defined as follows −

```
format EMPLOYEE_BOTTOM =

End of Page @<

        $%
```

Perl - File I/O

The basics of handling files are simple: you associate a **filehandle** with an external entity (usually a file) and then use a variety of operators and functions within Perl to read and update the data stored within the data stream associated with the filehandle.

A filehandle is a named internal Perl structure that associates a physical file with a name. All filehandles are capable of read/write access, so you can read from and update any file or device associated with a filehandle. However, when you associate a filehandle, you can specify the mode in which the filehandle is opened.

Three basic file handles are - **STDIN, STDOUT,** and **STDERR,**which represent standard input, standard output and standard error devices respectively.

Opening and Closing Files

There are following two functions with multiple forms, which can be used to open any new or existing file in Perl.

open FILEHANDLE, EXPR

open FILEHANDLE

sysopen FILEHANDLE, FILENAME, MODE, PERMS

sysopen FILEHANDLE, FILENAME, MODE

Here FILEHANDLE is the file handle returned by the **open**function and EXPR is the expression having file name and mode of opening the file.

Open Function:

Following is the syntax to open **file.txt** in read-only mode. Here less than < sign indicates that file has to be opend in read-only mode.

```
open(DATA, "<file.txt");
```

Here DATA is the file handle, which will be used to read the file. Here is the example, which will open a file and will print its content over the screen.

```
#!/usr/bin/perl

open(DATA, "<file.txt") or die "Couldn't open file file.txt, $!";

while(<DATA>) {

  print "$_";

}
```

Following is the syntax to open file.txt in writing mode. Here less than > sign indicates that file has to be opend in the writing mode.

```
open(DATA, ">file.txt") or die "Couldn't open file file.txt,
$!";
```

This example actually truncates (empties) the file before opening it for writing, which may not be the desired effect. If you want to open a file for reading and writing, you can put a plus sign before the > or < characters.

For example, to open a file for updating without truncating it –

```
open(DATA, "+<file.txt"); or die "Couldn't open file
file.txt, $!";
```

To truncate the file first –

```
open DATA, "+>file.txt" or die "Couldn't open file file.txt,
$!";
```

You can open a file in the append mode. In this mode, writing point will be set to the end of the file.

```
open(DATA,">>file.txt") || die "Couldn't open file file.txt,
$!";
```

A double >> opens the file for appending, placing the file pointer at the end, so that you can immediately start appending information. However, you can't read from it unless you also place a plus sign in front of it −

```
open(DATA,"+>>file.txt") || die "Couldn't open file file.txt,
$!";
```

Following is the table, which gives the possible values of different modes

Sr.No.	Entities & Definition
1	**< or r** Read Only Access
2	**> or w** Creates, Writes, and Truncates
3	**>> or a** Writes, Appends, and Creates
4	**+< or r+** Reads and Writes
5	**+> or w+**

	Reads, Writes, Creates, and Truncates
6	**+>> or a+**
	Reads, Writes, Appends, and Creates

Sysopen Function:

The **sysopen** function is similar to the main open function, except that it uses the system **open()** function, using the parameters supplied to it as the parameters for the system function –

For example, to open a file for updating, emulating the **+<filename** format from open –

```
sysopen(DATA, "file.txt", O_RDWR);
```

Or to truncate the file before updating –

```
sysopen(DATA, "file.txt", O_RDWR|O_TRUNC );
```

You can use O_CREAT to create a new file and O_WRONLY- to open file in write only mode and O_RDONLY - to open file in read only mode.

The **PERMS** argument specifies the file permissions for the file specified, if it has to be created. By default it takes **0x666**.

Following is the table, which gives the possible values of MODE.

Sr.No.	Entities & Definition
1	**O_RDWR** Read and Write
2	**O_RDONLY** Read Only
3	**O_WRONLY** Write Only
4	**O_CREAT** Create the file
5	**O_APPEND** Append the file
6	**O_TRUNC** Truncate the file

7	**O_EXCL**
	Stops if file already exists
8	**O_NONBLOCK**
	Non-Blocking usability

Close Function:

To close a filehandle, and therefore disassociate the filehandle from the corresponding file, you use the **close** function. This flushes the filehandle's buffers and closes the system's file descriptor.

```
close FILEHANDLE
close
```

If no FILEHANDLE is specified, then it closes the currently selected filehandle. It returns true only if it could successfully flush the buffers and close the file.

```
close(DATA) || die "Couldn't close file properly";
```

Reading and Writing Files

Once you have an open filehandle, you need to be able to read and write information. There are a number of different ways of reading and writing data into the file.

The <FILEHANDL> Operator

The main method of reading the information from an open filehandle is the <FILEHANDLE> operator. In a scalar context, it returns a single line from the filehandle. For example –

```
#!/usr/bin/perl


print "What is your name?\n";

$name = <STDIN>;

print "Hello $name\n";
```

When you use the <FILEHANDLE> operator in a list context, it returns a list of lines from the specified filehandle. For example, to import all the lines from a file into an array –

```
#!/usr/bin/perl


open(DATA,"<import.txt") or die "Can't open data";

@lines = <DATA>;

close(DATA);
```

getc Function:

The getc function returns a single character from the specified FILEHANDLE, or STDIN if none is specified –

```
getc FILEHANDLE

getc
```

If there was an error, or the filehandle is at end of file, then undef is returned instead.

read Function:

The read function reads a block of information from the buffered filehandle: This function is used to read binary data from the file.

```
read FILEHANDLE, SCALAR, LENGTH, OFFSET

read FILEHANDLE, SCALAR, LENGTH
```

The length of the data read is defined by LENGTH, and the data is placed at the start of SCALAR if no OFFSET is specified. Otherwise data is placed after OFFSET bytes in SCALAR. The function returns the number of bytes read on success, zero at end of file, or undef if there was an error.

print Function:

For all the different methods used for reading information from filehandles, the main function for writing information back is the print function.

```
print FILEHANDLE LIST

print LIST

print
```

The print function prints the evaluated value of LIST to FILEHANDLE, or to the current output filehandle (STDOUT by default). For example −

```
print "Hello World!\n";
```

Copying Files:

Here is the example, which opens an existing file file1.txt and read it line by line and generate another copy file file2.txt.

```
#!/usr/bin/perl


# Open file to read

open(DATA1, "<file1.txt");
```

```perl
# Open new file to write

open(DATA2, ">file2.txt");


# Copy data from one file to another.

while(<DATA1>) {

  print DATA2 $_;

}

close( DATA1 );

close( DATA2 );
```

Renaming a file:

Here is an example, which shows how we can rename a file file1.txt to file2.txt. Assuming file is available in /usr/test directory.

```perl
#!/usr/bin/perl


rename ("/usr/test/file1.txt", "/usr/test/file2.txt" );
```

This function **renames** takes two arguments and it just renames the existing file.

Deleting an Existing File:

Here is an example, which shows how to delete a file file1.txt using the **unlink** function.

```
#!/usr/bin/perl

unlink ("/usr/test/file1.txt");
```

Positioning inside a File:

You can use to **tell** function to know the current position of a file and **seek** function to point a particular position inside the file.

tell Function:

The first requirement is to find your position within a file, which you do using the tell function −

```
tell FILEHANDLE

tell
```

This returns the position of the file pointer, in bytes, within FILEHANDLE if specified, or the current default selected filehandle if none is specified.

seek Function:

The seek function positions the file pointer to the specified number of bytes within a file −

```
seek FILEHANDLE, POSITION, WHENCE
```

The function uses the fseek system function, and you have the same ability to position relative to three different points: the start, the end, and the current position. You do this by specifying a value for WHENCE.

Zero sets the positioning relative to the start of the file. For example, the line sets the file pointer to the 256th byte in the file.

```
seek DATA, 256, 0;
```

File Information:

You can test certain features very quickly within Perl using a series of test operators known collectively as -X tests. For example, to perform a quick test of the various permissions on a file, you might use a script like this −

```
#/usr/bin/perl

my $file = "/usr/test/file1.txt";
```

```perl
my (@description, $size);

if (-e $file) {

    push @description, 'binary' if (-B _);

    push @description, 'a socket' if (-S _);

    push @description, 'a text file' if (-T _);

    push @description, 'a block special file' if (-b _);

    push @description, 'a character special file' if (-c _);

    push @description, 'a directory' if (-d _);

    push @description, 'executable' if (-x _);

    push @description, (($size = -s _)) ? "$size bytes" : 'empty';

    print "$file is ", join(', ',@description),"\n";

}
```

Here is the list of features, which you can check for a file or directory −

Sr.No.	Operator & Definition
1	**-A** Script start time minus file last access time, in days.

2	**-B** Is it a binary file?
3	**-C** Script start time minus file last inode change time, in days.
3	**-M** Script start time minus file modification time, in days.
4	**-O** Is the file owned by the real user ID?
5	**-R** Is the file readable by the real user ID or real group?
6	**-S** Is the file a socket?
7	**-T**

		Is it a text file?
8	**-W**	Is the file writable by the real user ID or real group?
9	**-X**	Is the file executable by the real user ID or real group?
10	**-b**	Is it a block special file?
11	**-c**	Is it a character special file?
12	**-d**	Is the file a directory?
13	**-e**	Does the file exist?

14	**-f** Is it a plain file?
15	**-g** Does the file have the setgid bit set?
16	**-k** Does the file have the sticky bit set?
17	**-l** Is the file a symbolic link?
18	**-o** Is the file owned by the effective user ID?
19	**-p** Is the file a named pipe?
20	**-r** Is the file readable by the effective user or group ID?

21	-s Returns the size of the file, zero size = empty file.
22	-t Is the filehandle opened by a TTY (terminal)?
23	-u Does the file have the setuid bit set?
24	-w Is the file writable by the effective user or group ID?
25	-x Is the file executable by the effective user or group ID?
26	-z Is the file size zero?

Perl – Directories

Following are the standard functions used to play with directories.

```
opendir DIRHANDLE, EXPR  # To open a directory
readdir DIRHANDLE        # To read a directory
rewinddir DIRHANDLE      # Positioning pointer to the begining
telldir DIRHANDLE        # Returns current position of the dir
seekdir DIRHANDLE, POS   # Pointing pointer to POS inside dir
closedir DIRHANDLE       # Closing a directory.
```

Display all the Files:

There are various ways to list down all the files available in a particular directory. First let's use the simple way to get and list down all the files using the **glob** operator –

```perl
#!/usr/bin/perl


# Display all the files in /tmp directory.

$dir = "/tmp/*";

my @files = glob( $dir );


foreach (@files ) {
```

```perl
  print $_ . "\n";

}


# Display all the C source files in /tmp directory.

$dir = "/tmp/*.c";

@files = glob( $dir );


foreach (@files ) {

  print $_ . "\n";

}


# Display all the hidden files.

$dir = "/tmp/.*";

@files = glob( $dir );

foreach (@files ) {

  print $_ . "\n";

}


# Display all the files from /tmp and /home directories.
```

```perl
$dir = "/tmp/* /home/*";

@files = glob( $dir );


foreach (@files ) {

    print $_ . "\n";

}
```

Here is another example, which opens a directory and list out all the files available inside this directory.

```perl
#!/usr/bin/perl


opendir (DIR, '.') or die "Couldn't open directory, $!";

while ($file = readdir DIR) {

    print "$file\n";

}

closedir DIR;
```

One more example to print the list of C source files you might use is −

```perl
#!/usr/bin/perl
```

```perl
opendir(DIR, '.') or die "Couldn't open directory, $!";
foreach (sort grep(/^.*\.c$/,readdir(DIR))) {
  print "$_\n";
}
closedir DIR;
```

Create new Directory:

You can use **mkdir** function to create a new directory. You will need to have the required permission to create a directory.

```perl
#!/usr/bin/perl

$dir = "/tmp/perl";

# This creates perl directory in /tmp directory.
mkdir( $dir ) or die "Couldn't create $dir directory, $!";
print "Directory created successfully\n";
```

Remove a directory:

You can use **rmdir** function to remove a directory. You will need to have the required permission to remove a directory. Additionally this directory should be empty before you try to remove it.

```perl
#!/usr/bin/perl

$dir = "/tmp/perl";

# This removes perl directory from /tmp directory.

rmdir( $dir ) or die "Couldn't remove $dir directory, $!";

print "Directory removed successfully\n";
```

Change a Directory:

You can use **chdir** function to change a directory and go to a new location. You will need to have the required permission to change a directory and go inside the new directory.

```perl
#!/usr/bin/perl


$dir = "/home";


# This changes perl directory  and moves you inside /home
directory.

chdir( $dir ) or die "Couldn't go inside $dir directory, $!";

print "Your new location is $dir\n";
```

Perl - Error Handling

The execution and the errors always go together. If you are opening a file which does not exist. then if you did not handle this situation properly then your program is considered to be of bad quality.

The program stops if an error occurs. So a proper error handling is used to handle various type of errors, which may occur during a program execution and take appropriate action instead of halting program completely.

You can identify and trap an error in a number of different ways. Its very easy to trap errors in Perl and then handling them properly. Here are few methods which can be used.

The if statement

The **if statement** is the obvious choice when you need to check the return value from a statement; for example –

```perl
if(open(DATA, $file)) {

    ...

} else {

    die "Error: Couldn't open the file - $!";

}
```

Here variable $! returns the actual error message. Alternatively, we can reduce the statement to one line in situations where it makes sense to do so; for example –

```
open(DATA, $file) || die "Error: Couldn't open the file $!";
```

The unless Function

The **unless** function is the logical opposite to if: statements can completely bypass the success status and only be executed if the expression returns false. For example –

```
unless(chdir("/etc")) {

    die "Error: Can't change directory - $!";

}
```

The **unless** statement is best used when you want to raise an error or alternative only if the expression fails. The statement also makes sense when used in a single-line statement –

```
die    "Error:    Can't    change    directory!:    $!"
unless(chdir("/etc"));
```

Here we die only if the chdir operation fails, and it reads nicely.

The ternary Operator:

For very short tests, you can use the conditional operator **?:**

```
print(exists($hash{value}) ? 'There' : 'Missing',"\n");
```

It's not quite so clear here what we are trying to achieve, but the effect is the same as using an **if** or **unless** statement. The conditional operator is best used when you want to quickly return one of the two values within an expression or statement.

The warn Function:

The warn function just raises a warning, a message is printed to STDERR, but no further action is taken. So it is more useful if you just want to print a warning for the user and proceed with rest of the operation –

```
chdir('/etc') or warn "Can't change directory";
```

The die Function:

The die function works just like warn, except that it also calls exit. Within a normal script, this function has the effect of immediately terminating execution. You should use this function in case it is useless to proceed if there is an error in the program –

```
chdir('/etc') or die "Can't change directory";
```

Errors within Modules:

There are two different situations we should be able to handle –

- Reporting an error in a module that quotes the module's filename and line number - this is useful when debugging a module, or when you specifically want to raise a module-related, rather than script-related, error.

- Reporting an error within a module that quotes the caller's information so that you can debug the line within the script that caused the error. Errors raised in this fashion are useful to the end-user, because they highlight the error in relation to the calling script's origination line.

The **warn** and **die** functions work slightly differently than you would expect when called from within a module. For example, the simple module –

```
package T;


require Exporter;
@ISA = qw/Exporter/;
@EXPORT = qw/function/;
```

```
use Carp;

sub function {

  warn "Error in module!";

}

1;
```

When called from a script like below –

```
use T;

function();
```

It will produce the following result –

```
Error in module! at T.pm line 9.
```

This is more or less what you might expected, but not necessarily what you want. From a module programmer's perspective, the information is useful because it helps to point to a bug within the module itself. For an end-user, the information provided is fairly useless, and for all but the hardened programmer, it is completely pointless.

The solution for such problems is the Carp module, which provides a simplified method for reporting errors within modules that return information about the calling script.

The Carp module provides four functions: carp, cluck, croak, and confess. These functions are discussed below.

The carp Function:

The carp function is the basic equivalent of warn and prints the message to STDERR without actually exiting the script and printing the script name.

```
package T;


require Exporter;

@ISA = qw/Exporter/;

@EXPORT = qw/function/;

use Carp;

sub function {

  carp "Error in module!";

}

1;
```

When called from a script like below –

```
use T;

function();
```

It will produce the following result –

Error in module! at test.pl line 4

The cluck Function:

The cluck function is a sort of supercharged carp, it follows the same basic principle but also prints a stack trace of all the modules that led to the function being called, including the information on the original script.

```
package T;


require Exporter;

@ISA = qw/Exporter/;

@EXPORT = qw/function/;

use Carp qw(cluck);


sub function {

  cluck "Error in module!";

}

1;
```

When called from a script like below −

```
use T;

function();
```

It will produce the following result –

```
Error in module! at T.pm line 9
  T::function() called at test.pl line 4
```

The croak Function:

The **croak** function is equivalent to **die**, except that it reports the caller one level up. Like die, this function also exits the script after reporting the error to STDERR –

```
package T;


require Exporter;

@ISA = qw/Exporter/;

@EXPORT = qw/function/;

use Carp;


sub function {

  croak "Error in module!";

}

1;
```

When called from a script like below –

```
use T;

function();
```

It will produce the following result −

```
Error in module! at test.pl line 4
```

As with carp, the same basic rules apply regarding the including of line and file information according to the warn and die functions.

The confess Function:

The **confess** function is like **cluck**; it calls die and then prints a stack trace all the way up to the origination script.

```
package T;


require Exporter;

@ISA = qw/Exporter/;

@EXPORT = qw/function/;

use Carp;


sub function {

    confess "Error in module!";
```

```
}
1;
```

When called from a script like below –

```
use T;

function();
```

It will produce the following result –

```
Error in module! at T.pm line 9
   T::function() called at test.pl line 4
```

Perl - Special Variables

There are some variables which have a predefined and special meaning in Perl. They are the variables that use punctuation characters after the usual variable indicator ($, @, or %), such as $_ (explained below).

Most of the special variables have an english like long name, e.g., Operating System Error variable $! can be written as $OS_ERROR. But if you are going to use english like names, then you would have to put one line **use English;** at the top of your program file. This guides the interpreter to pickup exact meaning of the variable.

The most commonly used special variable is $_, which contains the default input and pattern-searching string. For example, in the following lines –

```perl
#!/usr/bin/perl


foreach ('hickory','dickory','doc') {

  print $_;

  print "\n";

}
```

When executed, this will produce the following result –

```
hickory
```

```
dickory
doc
```

Again, let's check the same example without using $_
variable explicitly −

```perl
#!/usr/bin/perl


foreach ('hickory','dickory','doc') {

  print;

  print "\n";

}
```

When executed, this will also produce the following result
−

```
hickory
dickory
doc
```

The first time the loop is executed, "hickory" is printed.
The second time around, "dickory" is printed, and the third
time, "doc" is printed. That's because in each iteration of
the loop, the current string is placed in $_, and is used by
default by print. Here are the places where Perl will
assume $_ even if you don't specify it −

- Various unary functions, including functions like ord and int, as well as the all file tests (-f, -d) except for -t, which defaults to STDIN.

- Various list functions like print and unlink.

- The pattern-matching operations m//, s///, and tr/// when used without an =~ operator.

- The default iterator variable in a foreach loop if no other variable is supplied.

- The implicit iterator variable in the grep and map functions.

- The default place to put an input record when a line-input operation's result is tested by itself as the sole criterion of a while test (i.e.,). Note that outside of a while test, this will not happen.

Special Variable Types:

Based on the usage and nature of special variables, we can categorize them in the following categories –

- Global Scalar Special Variables.
- Global Array Special Variables.
- Global Hash Special Variables.
- Global Special Filehandles.

- Global Special Constants.

- Regular Expression Special Variables.

- Filehandle Special Variables.

Global Scalar Special Variables:

Here is the list of all the scalar special variables. We have listed corresponding english like names along with the symbolic names.

$_ $ARG	The default input and pattern-searching space.
$. $NR	The current input line number of the last filehandle that was read. An explicit close on the filehandle resets the line number.

$/ $RS	The input record separator; newline by default. If set to the null string, it treats blank lines as delimiters.
$, $OFS	The output field separator for the print operator.
$\ $ORS	The output record separator for the print operator.
$" $LIST_SEPARATOR	Like "$," except that it applies to list values interpolated

	into a double-quoted string (or similar interpreted string). Default is a space.
$; $SUBSCRIPT_SEPARATOR	The subscript separator for multidimensional array emulation. Default is "\034".
$^L $FORMAT_FORMFEED	What a format outputs to perform a formfeed. Default is "\f".
$: $FORMAT_LINE_BREAK_CHARACT	The current set of characters after which a string may be broken to fill

ERS	continuation fields (starting with ^) in a format. Default is "\n"".
$^A $ACCUMULATOR	The current value of the write accumulator for format lines.
$# $OFMT	Contains the output format for printed numbers (deprecated).
$? $CHILD_ERROR	The status returned by the last pipe close, backtick (``) command, or system

	operator.
$! $OS_ERROR or $ERRNO	If used in a numeric context, yields the current value of the errno variable, identifying the last system call error. If used in a string context, yields the corresponding system error string.
$@ $EVAL_ERROR	The Perl syntax error message from the last eval command.
$$	The pid of the Perl process running this

$PROCESS_ID or $PID	script.
$<	The real user ID (uid) of this process.
$REAL_USER_ID or $UID	
$>	The effective user ID of this process.
$EFFECTIVE_USER_ID or $EUID	
$(	The real group ID (gid) of this process.
$REAL_GROUP_ID or $GID	
$)	The effective gid of this process.
$EFFECTIVE_GROUP_ID or $EGID	
$0	Contains the name of the file containing the Perl script

	being executed.
$PROGRAM_NAME	
$[	The index of the first element in an array and of the first character in a substring. Default is 0.
$]	Returns the version plus patchlevel divided by 1000.
$PERL_VERSION	
$^D	The current value of the debugging flags.
$DEBUGGING	

$^E $EXTENDED_OS_ERROR	Extended error message on some platforms.
$^F $SYSTEM_FD_MAX	The maximum system file descriptor, ordinarily 2.
$^H	Contains internal compiler hints enabled by certain pragmatic modules.
$^I $INPLACE_EDIT	The current value of the inplace-edit extension. Use undef to disable inplace

	editing.
$^M	The contents of $M can be used as an emergency memory pool in case Perl dies with an out-of-memory error. Use of $M requires a special compilation of Perl. See the INSTALL document for more information.
$^O	Contains the name of the
$OSNAME	operating system that the current Perl binary was

	compiled for.
$^P $PERLDB	The internal flag that the debugger clears so that it doesn't debug itself.
$^T $BASETIME	The time at which the script began running, in seconds since the epoch.
$^W $WARNING	The current value of the warning switch, either true or false.
$^X	The name that the Perl binary itself was

$EXECUTABLE_NAME	executed as.
$ARGV	Contains the name of the current file when reading from <ARGV>.

Global Array Special Variables:

@ARGV	The array containing the command-line arguments intended for the script.
@INC	The array containing the list of places to look for Perl scripts to be evaluated by the do, require, or use constructs.
@F	The array into which the input lines are split when the -a command-line switch is given.

Global Hash Special Variables:

%INC	The hash containing entries for the filename of each file that has been included via do or require.
%ENV	The hash containing your current environment.
%SIG	The hash used to set signal handlers for various signals.

Global Special Filehandles:

ARGV	The special filehandle that iterates over command line filenames in @ARGV. Usually written as the null filehandle in <>.
STDERR	The special filehandle for standard error in any package.
STDIN	The special filehandle for standard input in any package.

STDOUT	The special filehandle for standard output in any package.
DATA	The special filehandle that refers to anything following the __END__ token in the file containing the script. Or, the special filehandle for anything following the __DATA__ token in a required file, as long as you're reading data in the same package __DATA__ was found in.
_ (underscore)	The special filehandle used to cache the information from the last stat, lstat, or file test operator.

Global Special Constants:

__END__	Indicates the logical end of your program. Any following text is ignored, but may be read via the DATA filehandle.
__FILE__	Represents the filename at the point in your program where it's used. Not interpolated into strings.

__LINE__	Represents the current line number. Not interpolated into strings.
__PACKAGE__	Represents the current package name at compile time, or undefined if there is no current package. Not interpolated into strings.

Regular Expression Special Variables:

$digit	Contains the text matched by the corresponding set of parentheses in the last pattern matched. For example, $1 matches whatever was contained in the first set of parentheses in the previous regular expression.
$& $MATCH	The string matched by the last successful pattern match.
$`	The string preceding whatever was matched by the

$PREMATCH	last successful pattern match.
$' $POSTMATCH	The string following whatever was matched by the last successful pattern match.
$+ $LAST_PAREN_MATCH	The last bracket matched by the last search pattern. This is useful if you don't know which of a set of alternative patterns was matched. For example : /Version: (.*)|Revision: (.*)/ && ($rev = $+);

Filehandle Special Variables:

$| $OUTPUT_AUTOFLUSH	If set to nonzero, forces an fflush(3) after every write or print on the currently selected output channel.

$% $FORMAT_PAGE_NUMBER	The current page number of the currently selected output channel.
$= $FORMAT_LINES_PER_PAGE	The current page length (printable lines) of the currently selected output channel. Default is 60.
$- $FORMAT_LINES_LEFT	The number of lines left on the page of the currently selected output channel.
$~ $FORMAT_NAME	The name of the current report format for the currently selected output channel. Default is the name of the filehandle.
$^	The name of the current top-of-page

$FORMAT_TOP_NAME	format for the currently selected output channel. Default is the name of the filehandle with _TOP appended.

Perl - Coding Standard

Each programmer will, of course, have his or her own preferences in regards to formatting, but there are some general guidelines that will make your programs easier to read, understand, and maintain.

The most important thing is to run your programs under the -w flag at all times. You may turn it off explicitly for particular portions of code via the no warnings pragma or the $^W variable if you must. You should also always run under use strict or know the reason why not. The use sigtrap and even use diagnostics pragmas may also prove useful.

Regarding aesthetics of code lay out, about the only thing Larry cares strongly about is that the closing curly bracket of a multi-line BLOCK should line up with the keyword that started the construct. Beyond that, he has other preferences that aren't so strong −

- 4-column indent.
- Opening curly on same line as keyword, if possible, otherwise line up.
- Space before the opening curly of a multi-line BLOCK.
- One-line BLOCK may be put on one line, including curlies.
- No space before the semicolon.

- Semicolon omitted in "short" one-line BLOCK.

- Space around most operators.

- Space around a "complex" subscript (inside brackets).

- Blank lines between chunks that do different things.

- Uncuddled elses.

- No space between function name and its opening parenthesis.

- Space after each comma.

- Long lines broken after an operator (except and and or).

- Space after last parenthesis matching on current line.

- Line up corresponding items vertically.

- Omit redundant punctuation as long as clarity doesn't suffer.

Here are some other more substantive style issues to think about: Just because you CAN do something a particular way doesn't mean that you SHOULD do it that way. Perl is designed to give you several ways to do anything, so consider picking the most readable one. For instance –

```
open(FOO,$foo) || die "Can't open $foo: $!";
```

Is better than –

```
die "Can't open $foo: $!" unless open(FOO,$foo);
```

Because the second way hides the main point of the statement in a modifier. On the other hand,

```
print "Starting analysis\n" if $verbose;
```

Is better than –

```
$verbose && print "Starting analysis\n";
```

Because the main point isn't whether the user typed -v or not.

Don't go through silly contortions to exit a loop at the top or the bottom, when Perl provides the last operator so you can exit in the middle. Just "outdent" it a little to make it more visible –

```
LINE:

for (;;) {

    statements;

    last LINE if $foo;

    next LINE if /^#/;

    statements;

}
```

Let's see few more important points –

- Don't be afraid to use loop labels--they're there to enhance readability as well as to allow multilevel loop breaks. See the previous example.

- Avoid using grep() (or map()) or `backticks` in a void context, that is, when you just throw away their return values. Those functions all have return values, so use them. Otherwise use a foreach() loop or the system() function instead.

- For portability, when using features that may not be implemented on every machine, test the construct in an eval to see if it fails. If you know what version or patchlevel a particular feature was implemented, you can test $] ($PERL_VERSION in English) to see if it will be there. The Config module will also let you interrogate values determined by the Configure program when Perl was installed.

- Choose mnemonic identifiers. If you can't remember what mnemonic means, you've got a problem.

- While short identifiers like $gotit are probably ok, use underscores to separate words in longer identifiers. It is generally easier to read $var_names_like_this than $VarNamesLikeThis, especially for non-native speakers of English. It's also a simple rule that works consistently with VAR_NAMES_LIKE_THIS.

- Package names are sometimes an exception to this rule. Perl informally reserves lowercase module names for "pragma" modules like integer and strict. Other modules should begin with a capital letter and use mixed case, but probably without underscores due to limitations in primitive file systems' representations of module names as files that must fit into a few sparse bytes.

- If you have a really hairy regular expression, use the /x modifier and put in some whitespace to make it look a little less like line noise. Don't use slash as a delimiter when your regexp has slashes or backslashes.

- Always check the return codes of system calls. Good error messages should go to STDERR, include which program caused the problem, what the failed system call and arguments were, and (VERY IMPORTANT) should contain the standard system error message for what went wrong. Here's a simple but sufficient example –

```
opendir(D, $dir) or die "can't opendir $dir: $!";
```

- Think about reusability. Why waste brainpower on a one-shot when you might want to do something like it again? Consider generalizing your code. Consider writing a module or object class. Consider making your code run cleanly with use strict and use warnings (or -w) in effect. Consider giving away your code. Consider changing your whole world view. Consider... oh, never mind.

- Be consistent.

- Be nice.

Perl - Regular Expressions

A regular expression is a string of characters that defines the pattern or patterns you are viewing. The syntax of regular expressions in Perl is very similar to what you will find within other regular expression.supporting programs, such as **sed**, **grep**, and **awk**.

The basic method for applying a regular expression is to use the pattern binding operators =~ and !~. The first operator is a test and assignment operator.

There are three regular expression operators within Perl.

- Match Regular Expression - m//
- Substitute Regular Expression - s///
- Transliterate Regular Expression - tr///

The forward slashes in each case act as delimiters for the regular expression (regex) that you are specifying. If you are comfortable with any other delimiter, then you can use in place of forward slash.

The Match Operator:

The match operator, m//, is used to match a string or statement to a regular expression. For example, to match the character sequence "foo" against the scalar $bar, you might use a statement like this −

```
#!/usr/bin/perl
```

```perl
$bar = "This is foo and again foo";

if ($bar =~ /foo/) {

    print "First time is matching\n";

} else {

    print "First time is not matching\n";

}


$bar = "foo";

if ($bar =~ /foo/) {

    print "Second time is matching\n";

} else {

    print "Second time is not matching\n";

}
```

When above program is executed, it produces the following result –

```
First time is matching
Second time is matching
```

The m// actually works in the same fashion as the q// operator series.you can use any combination of naturally matching characters to act as delimiters for the expression. For example, m{}, m(), and m>< are all valid. So above example can be re-written as follows −

```
#!/usr/bin/perl


$bar = "This is foo and again foo";
if ($bar =~ m[foo]) {

   print "First time is matching\n";

} else {

   print "First time is not matching\n";

}


$bar = "foo";

if ($bar =~ m{foo}) {

   print "Second time is matching\n";

} else {

   print "Second time is not matching\n";

}
```

You can omit m from m// if the delimiters are forward slashes, but for all other delimiters you must use the m prefix.

Note that the entire match expression, that is the expression on the left of =~ or !~ and the match operator, returns true (in a scalar context) if the expression matches. Therefore the statement −

```
$true = ($foo =~ m/foo/);
```

will set $true to 1 if $foo matches the regex, or 0 if the match fails. In a list context, the match returns the contents of any grouped expressions. For example, when extracting the hours, minutes, and seconds from a time string, we can use −

```
my ($hours, $minutes, $seconds) = ($time =~ m/(\d+):(\d+):(\d+)/);
```

Match Operator Modifiers:

The match operator supports its own set of modifiers. The /g modifier allows for global matching. The /i modifier will make the match case insensitive. Here is the complete list of modifiers

Sr.No.	Modifier & Description
1	**i** Makes the match case insensitive.
2	**m** Specifies that if the string has newline or carriage return characters, the ^ and $ operators will now match against a newline boundary, instead of a string boundary.
3	**o** Evaluates the expression only once.
4	**s** Allows use of . to match a newline character.
5	**x** Allows you to use white space in the expression for clarity.
6	**g**

7	Globally finds all matches.
	cg
	Allows the search to continue even after a global match fails.

Matching Only Once:

There is also a simpler version of the match operator - the ?PATTERN? operator. This is basically identical to the m// operator except that it only matches once within the string you are searching between each call to reset.

For example, you can use this to get the first and last elements within a list –

```
#!/usr/bin/perl


@list = qw/food foosball subeo footnote terfoot canic
footbrdige/;


foreach (@list) {

  $first = $1 if /(foo.*?)/;

  $last = $1 if /(foo.*)/;
```

```
}
```

```
print "First: $first, Last: $last\n";
```

When above program is executed, it produces the following result −

First: foo, Last: footbrdige

Regular Expression Variables:

Regular expression variables include **$**, which contains whatever the last grouping match matched; **$&**, which contains the entire matched string; **$`**, which contains everything before the matched string; and **$'**, which contains everything after the matched string. Following code demonstrates the result −

```perl
#!/usr/bin/perl

$string = "The food is in the salad bar";
$string =~ m/foo/;
print "Before: $`\n";
print "Matched: $&\n";
print "After: $'\n";
```

When above program is executed, it produces the following result −

```
Before: The
Matched: foo
After: d is in the salad bar
```

The Substitution Operator:

The substitution operator, s///, is really just an extension of the match operator that allows you to replace the text matched with some new text. The basic form of the operator is −

```
s/PATTERN/REPLACEMENT/;
```

The PATTERN is the regular expression for the text that we are looking for. The REPLACEMENT is a specification for the text or regular expression that we want to use to replace the found text with. For example, we can replace all occurrences of **dog** with **cat** using the following regular expression −

```
#/user/bin/perl


$string = "The cat sat on the mat";

$string =~ s/cat/dog/;
```

```
print "$string\n";
```

When above program is executed, it produces the following result −

The dog sat on the mat

Substitution Operator Modifiers:

Here is the list of all the modifiers used with substitution operator.

Sr.No.	Modifier & Description
1	**i** Makes the match case insensitive.
2	**m** Specifies that if the string has newline or carriage return characters, the ^ and $ operators will now match against a newline boundary, instead of a string boundary.
3	**o** Evaluates the expression only once.

4	**s**
	Allows use of . to match a newline character.
5	**x**
	Allows you to use white space in the expression for clarity.
6	**g**
	Replaces all occurrences of the found expression with the replacement text.
7	**e**
	Evaluates the replacement as if it were a Perl statement, and uses its return value as the replacement text.

The Translation Operator:

Translation is similar, but not identical, to the principles of substitution, but unlike substitution, translation (or transliteration) does not use regular expressions for its search on replacement values. The translation operators are −

```
tr/SEARCHLIST/REPLACEMENTLIST/cds
y/SEARCHLIST/REPLACEMENTLIST/cds
```

The translation replaces all occurrences of the characters in SEARCHLIST with the corresponding characters in REPLACEMENTLIST. For example, using the "The cat sat on the mat." string we have been using in this chapter –

```
#/user/bin/perl

$string = 'The cat sat on the mat';
$string =~ tr/a/o/;


print "$string\n";
```

When above program is executed, it produces the following result –

The cot sot on the mot.

Standard Perl ranges can also be used, allowing you to specify ranges of characters either by letter or numerical value. To change the case of the string, you might use the following syntax in place of the **uc** function.

```
$string =~ tr/a-z/A-Z/;
```

Translation Operator Modifiers:

Following is the list of operators related to translation.

Sr.No.	Modifier & Description
1	c Complements SEARCHLIST.
2	d Deletes found but unreplaced characters.
3	s Squashes duplicate replaced characters.

The /d modifier deletes the characters matching SEARCHLIST that do not have a corresponding entry in REPLACEMENTLIST. For example −

```
#!/usr/bin/perl


$string = 'the cat sat on the mat.';

$string =~ tr/a-z/b/d;
```

```
print "$string\n";
```

When above program is executed, it produces the following result −

```
b b  b.
```

The last modifier, /s, removes the duplicate sequences of characters that were replaced, so −

```
#!/usr/bin/perl

$string = 'food';

$string = 'food';

$string =~ tr/a-z/a-z/s;


print "$string\n";
```

When above program is executed, it produces the following result −

```
fod
```

More Complex Regular Expressions:

You don't just have to match on fixed strings. In fact, you can match on just about anything you could dream of by using more complex regular expressions. Here's a quick cheat sheet –

Following table lists the regular expression syntax that is available in Python.

Sr.No.	Pattern & Description
1	^ Matches beginning of line.
2	$ Matches end of line.
3	. Matches any single character except newline. Using m option allows it to match newline as well.
4	[...] Matches any single character in brackets.

5	[^...] Matches any single character not in brackets.
6	* Matches 0 or more occurrences of preceding expression.
7	+ Matches 1 or more occurrence of preceding expression.
8	? Matches 0 or 1 occurrence of preceding expression.
9	{ n} Matches exactly n number of occurrences of preceding expression.
10	{ n,} Matches n or more occurrences of preceding expression.

11	**{ n, m}** Matches at least n and at most m occurrences of preceding expression.
12	**a| b** Matches either a or b.
13	**\w** Matches word characters.
14	**\W** Matches nonword characters.
15	**\s** Matches whitespace. Equivalent to [\t\n\r\f].
16	**\S** Matches nonwhitespace.
17	**\d** Matches digits. Equivalent to [0-9].

18	\D
	Matches nondigits.
19	\A
	Matches beginning of string.
20	\Z
	Matches end of string. If a newline exists, it matches just before newline.
21	\z
	Matches end of string.
22	\G
	Matches point where last match finished.
23	\b
	Matches word boundaries when outside brackets. Matches backspace (0x08) when inside brackets.
24	\B
	Matches nonword boundaries.

25	**\n, \t, etc.** Matches newlines, carriage returns, tabs, etc.
26	**\1...\9** Matches nth grouped subexpression.
27	**\10** Matches nth grouped subexpression if it matched already. Otherwise refers to the octal representation of a character code.
28	**[aeiou]** Matches a single character in the given set
29	**[^aeiou]** Matches a single character outside the given set

The ^ metacharacter matches the beginning of the string and the $ metasymbol matches the end of the string. Here are some brief examples.

```
# nothing in the string (start and end are adjacent)
/^$/
```

```
# a three digits, each followed by a whitespace

# character (eg "3 4 5 ")

/(\d\s) {3}/
```

```
# matches a string in which every

# odd-numbered letter is a (eg "abacadaf")

/(a.)+/
```

```
# string starts with one or more digits

/^\d+/
```

```
# string that ends with one or more digits

/\d+$/
```

Lets have a look at another example.

```
#!/usr/bin/perl
```

```
$string = "Cats go Catatonic\nWhen given Catnip";

($start) = ($string =~ /\A(.*?) /);
```

```
@lines = $string =~ /^(.*?) /gm;

print "First word: $start\n","Line starts: @lines\n";
```

When above program is executed, it produces the following result −

```
First word: Cats
Line starts: Cats When
```

Matching Boundaries:

The **\b** matches at any word boundary, as defined by the difference between the \w class and the \W class. Because \w includes the characters for a word, and \W the opposite, this normally means the termination of a word. The **\B** assertion matches any position that is not a word boundary. For example −

```
/\bcat\b/ # Matches 'the cat sat' but not 'cat on the mat'

/\Bcat\B/ # Matches 'verification' but not 'the cat on the mat'

/\bcat\B/ # Matches 'catatonic' but not 'polecat'

/\Bcat\b/ # Matches 'polecat' but not 'catatonic'
```

Selecting Alternatives:

The | character is just like the standard or bitwise OR within Perl. It specifies alternate matches within a regular expression or group. For example, to match "cat" or "dog" in an expression, you might use this −

```
if ($string =~ /cat|dog/)
```

You can group individual elements of an expression together in order to support complex matches. Searching for two people's names could be achieved with two separate tests, like this −

```
if (($string =~ /Martin Brown/) || ($string =~ /Sharon Brown/))
```

This could be written as follows

```
if ($string =~ /(Martin|Sharon) Brown/)
```

Grouping Matching:

From a regular-expression point of view, there is no difference between except, perhaps, that the former is slightly clearer.

```
$string =~ /(\S+)\s+(\S+)/;
```

and

```
$string =~ /\S+\s+\S+/;
```

However, the benefit of grouping is that it allows us to extract a sequence from a regular expression. Groupings are returned as a list in the order in which they appear in the original. For example, in the following fragment we have pulled out the hours, minutes, and seconds from a string.

```
my ($hours, $minutes, $seconds) = ($time =~ m/(\d+):(\d+):(\d+)/);
```

As well as this direct method, matched groups are also available within the special $x variables, where x is the number of the group within the regular expression. We could therefore rewrite the preceding example as follows –

```
#!/usr/bin/perl
```

```
$time = "12:05:30";
```

```perl
$time =~ m/(\d+):(\d+):(\d+)/;

my ($hours, $minutes, $seconds) = ($1, $2, $3);


print "Hours : $hours, Minutes: $minutes, Second: $seconds\n";
```

When above program is executed, it produces the following result –

Hours : 12, Minutes: 05, Second: 30

When groups are used in substitution expressions, the $x syntax can be used in the replacement text. Thus, we could reformat a date string using this –

```perl
#!/usr/bin/perl


$date = '03/26/1999';

$date =~ s#(\d+)/(\d+)/(\d+)#$3/$1/$2#;


print "$date\n";
```

When above program is executed, it produces the following result –

1999/03/26

The \G Assertion:

The \G assertion allows you to continue searching from the point where the last match occurred. For example, in the following code, we have used \G so that we can search to the correct position and then extract some information, without having to create a more complex, single regular expression –

```perl
#!/usr/bin/perl

$string = "The time is: 12:31:02 on 4/12/00";

$string =~ /:\s+/g;
($time) = ($string =~ /\G(\d+:\d+:\d+)/);
$string =~ /.+\s+/g;
($date) = ($string =~ m{\G(\d+/\d+/\d+)});

print "Time: $time, Date: $date\n";
```

When above program is executed, it produces the following result –

Time: 12:31:02, Date: 4/12/00

The \G assertion is actually just the metasymbol equivalent of the pos function, so between regular expression calls you can continue to use pos, and even modify the value of pos (and therefore \G) by using pos as an lvalue subroutine.

Regular-expression Examples:

Literal Characters

Sr.No.	Example & Description
1	**Perl** Match "Perl".

Character Classes

Sr.No.	Example & Description
1	**[Pp]ython** Matches "Python" or "python"
2	**rub[ye]** Matches "ruby" or "rube"
3	**[aeiou]**

	Matches any one lowercase vowel
4	**[0-9]** Matches any digit; same as [0123456789]
5	**[a-z]** Matches any lowercase ASCII letter
6	**[A-Z]** Matches any uppercase ASCII letter
7	**[a-zA-Z0-9]** Matches any of the above
8	**[^aeiou]** Matches anything other than a lowercase vowel
9	**[^0-9]** Matches anything other than a digit

Special Character Classes:

Sr.No.	Example & Description
1	. Matches any character except newline
2	\d Matches a digit: [0-9]
3	\D Matches a nondigit: [^0-9]
4	\s Matches a whitespace character: [\t\r\n\f]
5	\S Matches nonwhitespace: [^ \t\r\n\f]
6	\w Matches a single word character: [A-Za-z0-9_]

7	\W
	Matches a nonword character: [^A-Za-z0-9_]

Repetition Cases:

Sr.No.	Example & Description
1	**ruby?** Matches "rub" or "ruby": the y is optional
2	**ruby*** Matches "rub" plus 0 or more ys
3	**ruby+** Matches "rub" plus 1 or more ys
4	**\d{3}** Matches exactly 3 digits
5	**\d{3,}** Matches 3 or more digits

6.	\d{3,5}
	Matches 3, 4, or 5 digits

Nongreedy Repetition:

This matches the smallest number of repetitions –

Sr.No.	Example & Description
1	<.*>
	Greedy repetition: matches "<python>perl>"
2	<.*?>
	Nongreedy: matches "<python>" in "<python>perl>"

Grouping with Parentheses

Sr.No.	Example & Description
1	\D\d+
	No group: + repeats \d

2	**(\D\d)+** Grouped: + repeats \D\d pair
3	**([Pp]ython(,)?)+** Match "Python", "Python, python, python", etc.

Backreferences:

This matches a previously matched group again −

Sr.No.	Example & Description
1	**([Pp])ython&\1ails** Matches python&pails or Python&Pails
2	**(['"])[^\1]*\1** Single or double-quoted string. \1 matches whatever the 1st group matched. \2 matches whatever the 2nd group matched, etc.

Alternatives:

Sr.No.	Example & Description
1	**python|perl** Matches "python" or "perl"
2	**rub(y|le))** Matches "ruby" or "ruble"
3	**Python(!+|\?)** "Python" followed by one or more ! or one ?

Anchors:

This need to specify match positions.

Sr.No.	Example & Description
1	**^Python** Matches "Python" at the start of a string or internal line

2	**Python$** Matches "Python" at the end of a string or line
3	**\APython** Matches "Python" at the start of a string
4	**Python\Z** Matches "Python" at the end of a string
5	**\bPython\b** Matches "Python" at a word boundary
6	**\brub\B** \B is nonword boundary: match "rub" in "rube" and "ruby" but not alone
7	**Python(?=!)** Matches "Python", if followed by an exclamation point
8	**Python(?!!)** Matches "Python", if not followed by an

exclamation point

Special Syntax with Parentheses

Sr.No.	Example & Description
1	**R(?#comment)** Matches "R". All the rest is a comment
2	**R(?i)uby** Case-insensitive while matching "uby"
3	**R(?i:uby)** Same as above
4	**rub(?:y|le))** Group only without creating \1 backreference

Perl - Sending Email

Using sendmail Utility:

Sending a Plain Message

If you are working on Linux/Unix machine then you can simply use **sendmail** utility inside your Perl program to send email. Here is a sample script that can send an email to a given email ID. Just make sure the given path for sendmail utility is correct. This may be different for your Linux/Unix machine.

```
#!/usr/bin/perl


$to = 'abcd@gmail.com';

$from = 'webmaster@yourdomain.com';

$subject = 'Test Email';

$message = 'This is test email sent by Perl Script';


open(MAIL, "|/usr/sbin/sendmail -t");


# Email Header

print MAIL "To: $to\n";

print MAIL "From: $from\n";

print MAIL "Subject: $subject\n\n";
```

```perl
# Email Body

print MAIL $message;


close(MAIL);

print "Email Sent Successfully\n";
```

Actually, the above script is a client email script, which will draft email and submit to the server running locally on your Linux/Unix machine. This script will not be responsible for sending email to actual destination. So you have to make sure email server is properly configured and running on your machine to send email to the given email ID.

Sending an HTML Message:

If you want to send HTML formatted email using sendmail, then you simply need to add **Content-type: text/html\n** in the header part of the email as follows −

```perl
#!/usr/bin/perl


$to = 'abcd@gmail.com';

$from = 'webmaster@yourdomain.com';
```

```perl
$subject = 'Test Email';

$message = '<h1>This is test email sent by Perl Script</h1>';


open(MAIL, "|/usr/sbin/sendmail -t");


# Email Header

print MAIL "To: $to\n";

print MAIL "From: $from\n";

print MAIL "Subject: $subject\n\n";

print MAIL "Content-type: text/html\n";

# Email Body

print MAIL $message;


close(MAIL);

print "Email Sent Successfully\n";
```

Using MIME::Lite Module:

If you are working on windows machine, then you will not have access on sendmail utility. But you have alternate to write your own email client using MIME:Lite perl module. You can download this module from MIME-Lite-3.01.tar.gz and install it on your either machine Windows or Linux/Unix. To install it follow the simple steps –

```
$tar xvfz MIME-Lite-3.01.tar.gz

$cd MIME-Lite-3.01

$perl Makefile.PL

$make

$make install
```

That's it and you will have MIME::Lite module installed on your machine. Now you are ready to send your email with simple scripts explained below.

Sending a Plain Message:

Now following is a script which will take care of sending email to the given email ID –

```
#!/usr/bin/perl

use MIME::Lite;


$to = 'abcd@gmail.com';

$cc = 'efgh@mail.com';
```

```perl
$from = 'webmaster@yourdomain.com';

$subject = 'Test Email';

$message = 'This is test email sent by Perl Script';


$msg = MIME::Lite->new(

        From    => $from,

        To      => $to,

        Cc      => $cc,

        Subject => $subject,

        Data    => $message

        );


$msg->send;

print "Email Sent Successfully\n";
```

Sending an HTML Message:

If you want to send HTML formatted email using sendmail, then you simply need to add **Content-type: text/html\n** in the header part of the email. Following is the script, which will take care of sending HTML formatted email –

```perl
#!/usr/bin/perl

use MIME::Lite;


$to = 'abcd@gmail.com';

$cc = 'efgh@mail.com';

$from = 'webmaster@yourdomain.com';

$subject = 'Test Email';

$message = '<h1>This is test email sent by Perl Script</h1>';


$msg = MIME::Lite->new(

        From    => $from,

        To      => $to,

        Cc      => $cc,

        Subject => $subject,
```

```perl
        Data    => $message

        );
```

```perl
$msg->attr("content-type" => "text/html");

$msg->send;

print "Email Sent Successfully\n";
```

Sending an Attachment:

If you want to send an attachment, then following script serves the purpose –

```perl
#!/usr/bin/perl

use MIME::Lite;


$to = 'abcd@gmail.com';

$cc = 'efgh@mail.com';

$from = 'webmaster@yourdomain.com';

$subject = 'Test Email';

$message = 'This is test email sent by Perl Script';
```

```perl
$msg = MIME::Lite-=>new(

        From    => $from,

        To      => $to,

        Cc      => $cc,

        Subject => $subject,

        Type    => 'multipart/mixed'

        );
```

```perl
# Add your text message.

$msg->attach(Type      => 'text',

        Data        => $message

        );
```

```perl
# Specify your file as attachement.

$msg->attach(Type      => 'image/gif',

        Path        => '/tmp/logo.gif',

        Filename    => 'logo.gif',

        Disposition => 'attachment'

        );
```

```
$msg->send;

print "Email Sent Successfully\n";
```

You can attach as many files as you like in your email using attach() method.

Using SMTP Server:

If your machine is not running an email server then you can use any other email server available at the remote location. But to use any other email server you will need to have an id, its password, URL, etc. Once you have all the required information, you simple need to provide that information in **send()** method as follows –

```
$msg->send('smtp', "smtp.myisp.net", AuthUser=>"id", AuthPass=>"password" );
```

You can contact your email server administrator to have the above used information and if a user id and password is not already available then your administrator can create it in minutes.

Perl - Socket Programming

What is a Socket?

Socket is a Berkeley UNIX mechanism of creating a virtual duplex connection between different processes. This was later ported on to every known OS enabling communication between systems across geographical location running on different OS software. If not for the socket, most of the network communication between systems would never ever have happened.

Taking a closer look; a typical computer system on a network receives and sends information as desired by the various applications running on it. This information is routed to the system, since a unique IP address is designated to it. On the system, this information is given to the relevant applications, which listen on different ports. For example an internet browser listens on port 80 for information received from the web server. Also we can write our custom applications which may listen and send/receive information on a specific port number.

For now, let's sum up that a socket is an IP address and a port, enabling connection to send and recieve data over a network.

To explain above mentioned socket concept we will take an example of Client - Server Programming using Perl. To complete a client server architecture we would have to go through the following steps –

To Create a Server

- Create a socket using **socket** call.

- Bind the socket to a port address using **bind** call.

- Listen to the socket at the port address using **listen** call.

- Accept client connections using **accept** call.

To Create a Client

- Create a socket with **socket** call.

- Connect (the socket) to the server using **connect** call.

Following diagram shows the complete sequence of the calls used by Client and Server to communicate with each other –

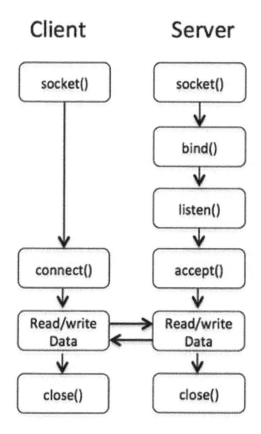

Server Side Socket Calls

The socket() call:

The **socket()** call is the first call in establishing a network connection is creating a socket. This call has the following syntax −

```
socket( SOCKET, DOMAIN, TYPE, PROTOCOL );
```

The above call creates a SOCKET and other three arguments are integers which should have the following values for TCP/IP connections.

- **DOMAIN** should be PF_INET. It's probable 2 on your computer.

- **TYPE** should be SOCK_STREAM for TCP/IP connection.

- **PROTOCOL** should be **(getprotobyname('tcp'))[2]**. It is the particular protocol such as TCP to be spoken over the socket.

So socket function call issued by the server will be something like this –

```
use Socket          # This defines PF_INET and
SOCK_STREAM


socket(SOCKET,PF_INET,SOCK_STREAM,(getprotobyname('tcp'))[2]);
```

The bind() call:

The sockets created by socket() call are useless until they are bound to a hostname and a port number. Server uses the following **bind()** function to specify the port at which they will be accepting connections from the clients.

```
bind( SOCKET, ADDRESS );
```

Here SOCKET is the descriptor returned by socket() call and ADDRESS is a socket address (for TCP/IP) containing three elements −

- The address family (For TCP/IP, that's AF_INET, probably 2 on your system).

- The port number (for example 21).

- The internet address of the computer (for example 10.12.12.168).

As the bind() is used by a server, which does not need to know its own address so the argument list looks like this −

```
use Socket              # This defines PF_INET and
SOCK_STREAM


$port = 12345;    # The unique port used by the sever to
listen requests

$server_ip_address = "10.12.12.168";

bind(        SOCKET,        pack_sockaddr_in($port,
inet_aton($server_ip_address)))

  or die "Can't bind to port $port! \n";
```

The **or die** clause is very important because if a server dies without outstanding connections, the port won't be immediately reusable unless you use the option SO_REUSEADDR using **setsockopt()** function. Here **pack_sockaddr_in()** function is being used to pack the Port and IP address into binary format.

The listen() call:

If this is a server program, then it is required to issue a call to **listen()** on the specified port to listen, i.e., wait for the incoming requests. This call has the following syntax –

```
listen( SOCKET, QUEUESIZE );
```

The above call uses SOCKET descriptor returned by socket() call and QUEUESIZE is the maximum number of outstanding connection request allowed simultaneously.

The accept() call:

If this is a server program then it is required to issue a call to the **access()** function to accept the incoming connections. This call has the following syntax –

```
accept( NEW_SOCKET, SOCKET );
```

The accept call receive SOCKET descriptor returned by socket() function and upon successful completion, a new socket descriptor NEW_SOCKET is returned for all future communication between the client and the server. If access() call fails, then it returns FLASE which is defined in Socket module which we have used initially.

Generally, accept() is used in an infinite loop. As soon as one connection arrives the server either creates a child process to deal with it or serves it himself and then goes back to listen for more connections.

```
while(1) {

  accept( NEW_SOCKET, SOCKT );

  .......
}
}
```

Now all the calls related to server are over and let us see a call which will be required by the client.

Client Side Socket Calls

The connect() call:

If you are going to prepare client program, then first you will use **socket()** call to create a socket and then you would have to use **connect()** call to connect to the server. You already have seen socket() call syntax and it will remain similar to server socket() call, but here is the syntax for **connect()** call −

```
connect( SOCKET, ADDRESS );
```

Here SCOKET is the socket descriptor returned by socket() call issued by the client and ADDRESS is a socket address similar to *bind* call, except that it contains the IP address of the remote server.

```
$port = 21;   # For example, the ftp port

$server_ip_address = "10.12.12.168";

connect(       SOCKET,        pack_sockaddr_in($port,
inet_aton($server_ip_address)))

  or die "Can't connect to port $port! \n";
```

If you connect to the server successfully, then you can start sending your commands to the server using SOCKET descriptor, otherwise your client will come out by giving an error message.

Client - Server Example:

Following is a Perl code to implement a simple client-server program using Perl socket. Here server listens for incoming requests and once connection is established, it simply replies *Smile from the server*. The client reads that message and print on the screen. Let's see how it has been done, assuming we have our server and client on the same machine.

Script to Create a Server

```perl
#!/usr/bin/perl -w
# Filename : server.pl

use strict;
use Socket;

# use port 7890 as default
my $port = shift || 7890;
my $proto = getprotobyname('tcp');
my $server = "localhost";  # Host IP running the server

# create a socket, make it reusable
socket(SOCKET, PF_INET, SOCK_STREAM, $proto)
    or die "Can't open socket $!\n";
setsockopt(SOCKET, SOL_SOCKET, SO_REUSEADDR, 1)
    or die "Can't set socket option to SO_REUSEADDR $!\n";
```

```perl
# bind to a port, then listen

bind(          SOCKET,          pack_sockaddr_in($port,
inet_aton($server)))

  or die "Can't bind to port $port! \n";


listen(SOCKET, 5) or die "listen: $!";

print "SERVER started on port $port\n";


# accepting a connection

my $client_addr;

while ($client_addr = accept(NEW_SOCKET, SOCKET))
{

  # send them a message, close connection

  my $name = gethostbyaddr($client_addr, AF_INET );

  print NEW_SOCKET "Smile from the server";

  print "Connection recieved from $name\n";

  close NEW_SOCKET;

}
```

To run the server in background mode issue the following command on Unix prompt −

```perl
$perl sever.pl&
```

Script to Create a Client

```perl
!/usr/bin/perl -w
# Filename : client.pl


use strict;
use Socket;


# initialize host and port
my $host = shift || 'localhost';
my $port = shift || 7890;
my $server = "localhost";  # Host IP running the server


# create the socket, connect to the port
socket(SOCKET,PF_INET,SOCK_STREAM,(getprotobyname('tcp'))[2])
  or die "Can't create a socket $!\n";
connect(       SOCKET,       pack_sockaddr_in($port,
inet_aton($server)))
  or die "Can't connect to port $port! \n";
```

```
my $line;

while ($line = <SOCKET>) {

  print "$line\n";

}

close SOCKET or die "close: $!";
```

Now let's start our client at the command prompt, which will connect to the server and read message sent by the server and displays the same on the screen as follows –

```
$perl client.pl

Smile from the server
```

NOTE – If you are giving the actual IP address in dot notation, then it is recommended to provide IP address in the same format in both client as well as server to avoid any confusion.

Object Oriented Programming in PERL:

We have already studied references in Perl and Perl anonymous arrays and hashes. Object Oriented concept in Perl is very much based on references and anonymous array and hashes. Let's start learning basic concepts of Object Oriented Perl.

Object Basics:

There are three main terms, explained from the point of view of how Perl handles objects. The terms are object, class, and method.

- An **object** within Perl is merely a reference to a data type that knows what class it belongs to. The object is stored as a reference in a scalar variable. Because a scalar only contains a reference to the object, the same scalar can hold different objects in different classes.

- A **class** within Perl is a package that contains the corresponding methods required to create and manipulate objects.

- A **method** within Perl is a subroutine, defined with the package. The first argument to the method is an object reference or a package name, depending on whether the method affects the current object or the class.

Perl provides a **bless()** function, which is used to return a reference which ultimately becomes an object.

Defining a Class:

It is very simple to define a class in Perl. A class is corresponding to a Perl Package in its simplest form. To create a class in Perl, we first build a package.

A package is a self-contained unit of user-defined variables and subroutines, which can be re-used over and over again.

Perl Packages provide a separate namespace within a Perl program which keeps subroutines and variables independent from conflicting with those in other packages.

To declare a class named Person in Perl we do −

```
package Person;
```

The scope of the package definition extends to the end of the file, or until another package keyword is encountered.

Creating and Using Objects:

To create an instance of a class (an object) we need an object constructor. This constructor is a method defined within the package. Most programmers choose to name this object constructor method new, but in Perl you can use any name.

You can use any kind of Perl variable as an object in Perl. Most Perl programmers choose either references to arrays or hashes.

Let's create our constructor for our Person class using a Perl hash reference. When creating an object, you need to supply a constructor, which is a subroutine within a package that returns an object reference. The object reference is created by blessing a reference to the package's class. For example –

```perl
package Person;
sub new {
   my $class = shift;
   my $self = {
     _firstName => shift,
     _lastName  => shift,
     _ssn       => shift,
   };
   # Print all the values just for clarification.
   print "First Name is $self->{_firstName}\n";
   print "Last Name is $self->{_lastName}\n";
   print "SSN is $self->{_ssn}\n";
```

```
bless $self, $class;

return $self;

}
```

Now Let us see how to create an Object.

```
$object = new Person( "Mohammad", "Saleem",
23234345);
```

You can use simple hash in your consturctor if you don't want to assign any value to any class variable. For example –

```
package Person;
sub new {
   my $class = shift;
   my $self = {};
   bless $self, $class;
   return $self;
}
```

Defining Methods:

Other object-oriented languages have the concept of security of data to prevent a programmer from changing an object data directly and they provide accessor methods to modify object data. Perl does not have private variables but we can still use the concept of helper methods to manipulate object data.

Lets define a helper method to get person's first name –

```perl
sub getFirstName {

  return $self->{_firstName};

}
```

Another helper function to set person's first name –

```perl
sub setFirstName {

  my ( $self, $firstName ) = @_;

  $self->{_firstName}          =          $firstName          if
defined($firstName);

  return $self->{_firstName};

}
```

Now lets have a look into complete example: Keep Person package and helper functions into Person.pm file.

```perl
#!/usr/bin/perl


package Person;


sub new {
  my $class = shift;
  my $self = {
    _firstName => shift,
    _lastName  => shift,
    _ssn       => shift,
  };
  # Print all the values just for clarification.
  print "First Name is $self->{_firstName}\n";
  print "Last Name is $self->{_lastName}\n";
  print "SSN is $self->{_ssn}\n";
  bless $self, $class;
  return $self;
}
sub setFirstName {
```

```perl
my ( $self, $firstName ) = @_;

$self->{_firstName}          =          $firstName          if
defined($firstName);

return $self->{_firstName};

}


sub getFirstName {

my( $self ) = @_;

return $self->{_firstName};

}

1;
```

Now let's make use of Person object in employee.pl file as follows −

```perl
#!/usr/bin/perl



use Person;



$object  =  new  Person(  "Mohammad",  "Saleem",
23234345);

# Get first name which is set using constructor.
```

```perl
$firstName = $object->getFirstName();


print "Before Setting First Name is : $firstName\n";


# Now Set first name using helper function.

$object->setFirstName( "Mohd." );


# Now get first name set by helper function.

$firstName = $object->getFirstName();

print "Before Setting First Name is : $firstName\n";
```

When we execute above program, it produces the following result –

```
First Name is Mohammad
Last Name is Saleem
SSN is 23234345
Before Setting First Name is : Mohammad
Before Setting First Name is : Mohd.
```

Inheritance:

Object-oriented programming has very good and useful concept called inheritance. Inheritance simply means that properties and methods of a parent class will be available to the child classes. So you don't have to write the same code again and again, you can just inherit a parent class.

For example, we can have a class Employee, which inherits from Person. This is referred to as an "isa" relationship because an employee is a person. Perl has a special variable, @ISA, to help with this. @ISA governs (method) inheritance.

Following are the important points to be considered while using inheritance −

- Perl searches the class of the specified object for the given method or attribute, i.e., variable.

- Perl searches the classes defined in the object class's @ISA array.

- If no method is found in steps 1 or 2, then Perl uses an AUTOLOAD subroutine, if one is found in the @ISA tree.

- If a matching method still cannot be found, then Perl searches for the method within the UNIVERSAL class (package) that comes as part of the standard Perl library.

- If the method still has not found, then Perl gives up and raises a runtime exception.

So to create a new Employee class that will inherit methods and attributes from our Person class, we simply code as follows: Keep this code into Employee.pm.

```perl
#!/usr/bin/perl


package Employee;

use Person;

use strict;

our @ISA = qw(Person);   # inherits from Person
```

Now Employee Class has all the methods and attributes inherited from Person class and you can use them as follows: Use main.pl file to test it −

```perl
#!/usr/bin/perl


use Employee;


$object = new Employee( "Mohammad", "Saleem", 23234345);
# Get first name which is set using constructor.
$firstName = $object->getFirstName();
```

```
print "Before Setting First Name is : $firstName\n";


# Now Set first name using helper function.

$object->setFirstName( "Mohd." );


# Now get first name set by helper function.

$firstName = $object->getFirstName();

print "After Setting First Name is : $firstName\n";
```

When we execute above program, it produces the following result −

```
First Name is Mohammad
Last Name is Saleem
SSN is 23234345
Before Setting First Name is : Mohammad
Before Setting First Name is : Mohd.
```

Method Overriding:

The child class Employee inherits all the methods from the parent class Person. But if you would like to override those methods in your child class then you can do it by giving your own implementation. You can add your additional functions in child class or you can add or modify the functionality of an existing methods in its parent class. It can be done as follows: modify Employee.pm file.

```perl
#!/usr/bin/perl


package Employee;
use Person;
use strict;
our @ISA = qw(Person);   # inherits from Person


# Override constructor
sub new {
  my ($class) = @_;


  # Call the constructor of the parent class, Person.
  my $self = $class->SUPER::new( $_[1], $_[2], $_[3] );
  # Add few more attributes
  $self->{_id}   = undef;
  $self->{_title} = undef;
```

```perl
    bless $self, $class;

    return $self;

}


# Override helper function

sub getFirstName {

    my( $self ) = @_;

    # This is child class function.

    print "This is child class helper function\n";

    return $self->{_firstName};

}


# Add more methods

sub setLastName{

    my ( $self, $lastName ) = @_;

    $self->{_lastName} = $lastName if defined($lastName);

    return $self->{_lastName};

}
```

```perl
sub getLastName {

  my( $self ) = @_;

  return $self->{_lastName};

}



1;
```

Now let's again try to use Employee object in our main.pl file and execute it.

```perl
#!/usr/bin/perl



use Employee;

$object = new Employee( "Mohammad", "Saleem", 23234345);

# Get first name which is set using constructor.

$firstName = $object->getFirstName();



print "Before Setting First Name is : $firstName\n";



# Now Set first name using helper function.
```

```
$object->setFirstName( "Mohd." );

# Now get first name set by helper function.

$firstName = $object->getFirstName();

print "After Setting First Name is : $firstName\n";
```

When we execute above program, it produces the following result –

```
First Name is Mohammad
Last Name is Saleem
SSN is 23234345
This is child class helper function
Before Setting First Name is : Mohammad
This is child class helper function
After Setting First Name is : Mohd.
```

Default Autoloading:

Perl offers a feature which you would not find in any other programming languages: a default subroutine. Which means, if you define a function called **AUTOLOAD(),** then any calls to undefined subroutines will call AUTOLOAD() function automatically. The name of the missing subroutine is accessible within this subroutine as $AUTOLOAD.

Default autoloading functionality is very useful for error handling. Here is an example to implement AUTOLOAD, you can implement this function in your own way.

```perl
sub AUTOLOAD {

  my $self = shift;

  my $type = ref ($self) || croak "$self is not an object";

  my $field = $AUTOLOAD;

  $field =~ s/.*:://;

  unless (exists $self->{$field}) {

    croak "$field does not exist in object/class $type";

  }
  if (@_) {

    return $self->($name) = shift;

  } else {

    return $self->($name);

  }

}
```

Destructors and Garbage Collection:

If you have programmed using object oriented programming before, then you will be aware of the need to create a **destructor** to free the memory allocated to the object when you have finished using it. Perl does this automatically for you as soon as the object goes out of scope.

In case you want to implement your destructor, which should take care of closing files or doing some extra processing then you need to define a special method called **DESTROY**. This method will be called on the object just before Perl frees the memory allocated to it. In all other respects, the DESTROY method is just like any other method, and you can implement whatever logic you want inside this method.

A destructor method is simply a member function (subroutine) named DESTROY, which will be called automatically in following cases −

- When the object reference's variable goes out of scope.
- When the object reference's variable is undef-ed.
- When the script terminates
- When the perl interpreter terminates

For Example, you can simply put the following method DESTROY in your class −

```
package MyClass;

...

sub DESTROY {

  print "MyClass::DESTROY called\n";
```

```
}
```

Object Oriented Perl Example:

Here is another nice example, which will help you to understand Object Oriented Concepts of Perl. Put this source code into any perl file and execute it.

```perl
#!/usr/bin/perl


# Following is the implementation of simple Class.

package MyClass;


sub new {

   print "MyClass::new called\n";

   my $type = shift;        # The package/type name

   my $self = {};           # Reference to empty hash

   return bless $self, $type;

}


sub DESTROY {

   print "MyClass::DESTROY called\n";
```

```perl
}


sub MyMethod {

  print "MyClass::MyMethod called!\n";

}



# Following is the implemnetation of Inheritance.
package MySubClass;


@ISA = qw( MyClass );


sub new {
  print "MySubClass::new called\n";
  my $type = shift;         # The package/type name
  my $self = MyClass->new;    # Reference to empty hash
  return bless $self, $type;
}
```

```perl
sub DESTROY {

  print "MySubClass::DESTROY called\n";

}


sub MyMethod {

  my $self = shift;

  $self->SUPER::MyMethod();

  print "  MySubClass::MyMethod called!\n";

}


# Here is the main program using above classes.

package main;


print "Invoke MyClass method\n";


$myObject = MyClass->new();

$myObject->MyMethod();


print "Invoke MySubClass method\n";
```

```
$myObject2 = MySubClass->new();

$myObject2->MyMethod();


print "Create a scoped object\n";

{

    my $myObject2 = MyClass->new();

}
# Destructor is called automatically here


print "Create and undef an object\n";

$myObject3 = MyClass->new();

undef $myObject3;


print "Fall off the end of the script...\n";

# Remaining destructors are called automatically here
```

When we execute above program, it produces the following result –

```
Invoke MyClass method
MyClass::new called
```

```
MyClass::MyMethod called!
Invoke MySubClass method
MySubClass::new called
MyClass::new called
MyClass::MyMethod called!
MySubClass::MyMethod called!
Create a scoped object
MyClass::new called
MyClass::DESTROY called
Create and undef an object
MyClass::new called
MyClass::DESTROY called
Fall off the end of the script...
MyClass::DESTROY called
MySubClass::DESTROY called
```

Perl - Database Access

This chapter teaches you how to access a database inside your Perl script. Starting from Perl 5 has become very easy to write database applications using **DBI** module. DBI stands for **Database Independent Interface** for Perl, which means DBI provides an abstraction layer between the Perl code and the underlying database, allowing you to switch database implementations really easily.

The DBI is a database access module for the Perl programming language. It provides a set of methods, variables, and conventions that provide a consistent database interface, independent of the actual database being used.

Architecture of a DBI Application:

DBI is independent of any database available in backend. You can use DBI whether you are working with Oracle, MySQL or Informix, etc. This is clear from the following architure diagram.

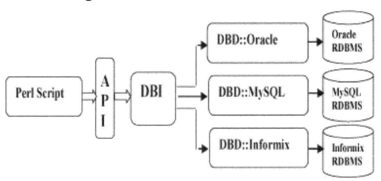

Here DBI is responsible of taking all SQL commands through the API, (i.e., Application Programming Interface) and to dispatch them to the appropriate driver for actual execution. And finally, DBI is responsible of taking results from the driver and giving back it to the calling scritp.

Notation and Conventions:

Throughout this chapter following notations will be used and it is recommended that you should also follow the same convention.

```
$dsn    Database source name
$dbh    Database handle object
$sth    Statement handle object
$h      Any of the handle types above ($dbh, $sth, or $drh)
$rc     General Return Code  (boolean: true=ok, false=error)
$rv     General Return Value (typically an integer)
@ary    List of values returned from the database.
$rows   Number of rows processed (if available, else -1)
$fh     A filehandle
undef   NULL values are represented by undefined values
in Perl
\%attr  Reference to a hash of attribute values passed to
methods
```

Database Connection:

Assuming we are going to work with MySQL database. Before connecting to a database make sure of the followings. You can take help of our MySQL tutorial in case you are not aware about how to create database and tables in MySQL database.

- You have created a database with a name TESTDB.

- You have created a table with a name TEST_TABLE in TESTDB.

- This table is having fields FIRST_NAME, LAST_NAME, AGE, SEX and INCOME.

- User ID "testuser" and password "test123" are set to access TESTDB.

- Perl Module DBI is installed properly on your machine.

- You have gone through MySQL tutorial to understand MySQL Basics.

Following is the example of connecting with MySQL database "TESTDB" –

```
#!/usr/bin/perl

use DBI

use strict;

my $driver = "mysql";
```

```
my $database = "TESTDB";

my $dsn = "DBI:$driver:database=$database";

my $userid = "testuser";

my $password = "test123";


my $dbh = DBI->connect($dsn, $userid, $password ) or die
$DBI::errstr;
```

If a connection is established with the datasource then a Database Handle is returned and saved into $dbh for further use otherwise $dbh is set to *undef* value and $DBI::errstr returns an error string.

INSERT Operation:

INSERT operation is required when you want to create some records into a table. Here we are using table TEST_TABLE to create our records. So once our database connection is established, we are ready to create records into TEST_TABLE. Following is the procedure to create single record into TEST_TABLE. You can create as many as records you like using the same concept.

Record creation takes the following steps –

- Preparing SQL statement with INSERT statement. This will be done using **prepare()** API.

- Executing SQL query to select all the results from the database. This will be done using **execute()** API.

- Releasing Stattement handle. This will be done using **finish()** API.

- If everything goes fine then **commit** this operation otherwise you can **rollback** complete transaction. Commit and Rollback are explained in next sections.

```
my $sth = $dbh->prepare("INSERT INTO TEST_TABLE

          (FIRST_NAME, LAST_NAME, SEX, AGE,
INCOME )

              values

              ('john', 'poul', 'M', 30, 13000)");

$sth->execute() or die $DBI::errstr;

$sth->finish();

$dbh->commit or die $DBI::errstr;
```

Using Bind Values:

There may be a case when values to be entered is not given in advance. So you can use bind variables which will take the required values at run time. Perl DBI modules make use of a question mark in place of actual value and then actual values are passed through execute() API at the run time. Following is the example –

```
my $first_name = "john";

my $last_name = "poul";

my $sex = "M";

my $income = 13000;

my $age = 30;

my $sth = $dbh->prepare("INSERT INTO TEST_TABLE

            (FIRST_NAME,   LAST_NAME,   SEX,
AGE, INCOME )

        values

        (?,?,?,?)");

$sth->execute($first_name,$last_name,$sex,        $age,
$income)

    or die $DBI::errstr;

$sth->finish();

$dbh->commit or die $DBI::errstr;
```

READ Operation:

READ Operation on any databasse means to fetch some useful information from the database, i.e., one or more records from one or more tables. So once our database connection is established, we are ready to make a query into this database. Following is the procedure to query all the records having AGE greater than 20. This will take four steps −

- Preparing SQL SELECT query based on required conditions. This will be done using **prepare()** API.

- Executing SQL query to select all the results from the database. This will be done using **execute()** API.

- Fetching all the results one by one and printing those results.This will be done using **fetchrow_array()** API.

- Releasing Stattement handle. This will be done using **finish()** API.

```
my  $sth  =  $dbh->prepare("SELECT  FIRST_NAME,
LAST_NAME

              FROM TEST_TABLE

              WHERE AGE > 20");
```

```
$sth->execute() or die $DBI::errstr;

print "Number of rows found :" + $sth->rows;

while (my @row = $sth->fetchrow_array()) {

  my ($first_name, $last_name ) = @row;

  print "First Name = $first_name, Last Name =
$last_name\n";

}

$sth->finish();
```

Using Bind Values:

There may be a case when condition is not given in advance. So you can use bind variables, which will take the required values at run time. Perl DBI modules makes use of a question mark in place of actual value and then the actual values are passed through execute() API at the run time. Following is the example –

```
$age = 20;

my $sth = $dbh->prepare("SELECT FIRST_NAME,
LAST_NAME

            FROM TEST_TABLE

            WHERE AGE > ?");
```

```
$sth->execute( $age ) or die $DBI::errstr;

print "Number of rows found :" + $sth->rows;

while (my @row = $sth->fetchrow_array()) {

  my ($first_name, $last_name ) = @row;

  print "First Name = $first_name, Last Name =
$last_name\n";

}

$sth->finish();
```

UPDATE Operation:

UPDATE Operation on any database means to update one or more records already available in the database tables. Following is the procedure to update all the records having SEX as 'M'. Here we will increase AGE of all the males by one year. This will take three steps −

- Preparing SQL query based on required conditions. This will be done using **prepare()** API.

- Executing SQL query to select all the results from the database. This will be done using **execute()** API.

- Releasing Stattement handle. This will be done using **finish()** API.

- If everything goes fine then **commit** this operation otherwise you can **rollback** complete transaction. See next section for commit and rollback APIs.

```perl
my $sth = $dbh->prepare("UPDATE TEST_TABLE

                SET   AGE = AGE + 1

                WHERE SEX = 'M'");

$sth->execute() or die $DBI::errstr;

print "Number of rows updated :" + $sth->rows;

$sth->finish();

$dbh->commit or die $DBI::errstr;
```

Using Bind Values:

There may be a case when condition is not given in advance. So you can use bind variables, which will take required values at run time. Perl DBI modules make use of a question mark in place of actual value and then the actual values are passed through execute() API at the run time. Following is the example –

```perl
$sex = 'M';

my $sth = $dbh->prepare("UPDATE TEST_TABLE

                SET   AGE = AGE + 1
```

```
                WHERE SEX = ?");

$sth->execute('$sex') or die $DBI::errstr;

print "Number of rows updated :" + $sth->rows;

$sth->finish();

$dbh->commit or die $DBI::errstr;
```

In some case you would like to set a value, which is not given in advance so you can use binding value as follows. In this example income of all males will be set to 10000.

```
$sex = 'M';

$income = 10000;

my $sth = $dbh->prepare("UPDATE TEST_TABLE

                SET   INCOME = ?

                WHERE SEX = ?");

$sth->execute( $income, '$sex') or die $DBI::errstr;

print "Number of rows updated :" + $sth->rows;

$sth->finish();
```

DELETE Operation:

DELETE operation is required when you want to delete some records from your database. Following is the procedure to delete all the records from TEST_TABLE where AGE is equal to 30. This operation will take the following steps.

- Preparing SQL query based on required conditions. This will be done using **prepare()** API.

- Executing SQL query to delete required records from the database. This will be done using **execute()** API.

- Releasing Stattement handle. This will be done using **finish()** API.

- If everything goes fine then **commit** this operation otherwise you can **rollback** complete transaction.

```
$age = 30;

my    $sth    =    $dbh->prepare("DELETE    FROM
TEST_TABLE

            WHERE AGE = ?");

$sth->execute( $age ) or die $DBI::errstr;
```

```
print "Number of rows deleted :" + $sth->rows;

$sth->finish();

$dbh->commit or die $DBI::errstr;
```

Using do Statement:

If you're doing an UPDATE, INSERT, or DELETE there is no data that comes back from the database, so there is a short cut to perform this operation. You can use **do** statement to execute any of the command as follows.

```
$dbh->do('DELETE FROM TEST_TABLE WHERE age =30');
```

do returns a true value if it succeeded, and a false value if it failed. Actually, if it succeeds it returns the number of affected rows. In the example it would return the number of rows that were actually deleted.

COMMIT Operation:

Commit is the operation which gives a green signal to database to finalize the changes and after this operation no change can be reverted to its orignal position.

Here is a simple example to call **commit** API.

```
$dbh->commit or die $dbh->errstr;
```

ROLLBACK Operation:

If you are not satisfied with all the changes or you encounter an error in between of any operation , you can revert those changes to use **rollback** API.

Here is a simple example to call **rollback** API.

```
$dbh->rollback or die $dbh->errstr;
```

Begin Transaction:

Many databases support transactions. This means that you can make a whole bunch of queries which would modify the databases, but none of the changes are actually made. Then at the end, you issue the special SQL query **COMMIT**, and all the changes are made simultaneously. Alternatively, you can issue the query ROLLBACK, in which case all the changes are thrown away and database remains unchanged.

Perl DBI module provided **begin_work** API, which enables transactions (by turning AutoCommit off) until the next call to commit or rollback. After the next commit or rollback, AutoCommit will automatically be turned on again.

```
$rc = $dbh->begin_work  or die $dbh->errstr;
```

AutoCommit Option:

If your transactions are simple, you can save yourself the trouble of having to issue a lot of commits. When you make the connect call, you can specify an **AutoCommit** option which will perform an automatic commit operation after every successful query. Here's what it looks like –

```
my $dbh = DBI->connect($dsn, $userid, $password,

        {AutoCommit => 1})

        or die $DBI::errstr;
```

Here AutoCommit can take value 1 or 0, where 1 means AutoCommit is on and 0 means AutoCommit is off.

Automatic Error Handling:

When you make the connect call, you can specify a RaiseErrors option that handles errors for you automatically. When an error occurs, DBI will abort your program instead of returning a failure code. If all you want is to abort the program on an error, this can be convenient. Here's what it looks like –

```
my $dbh = DBI->connect($dsn, $userid, $password,

        {RaiseError => 1})
```

```
or die $DBI::errstr;
```

Here RaiseError can take value 1 or 0.

Disconnecting Database:

To disconnect Database connection, use **disconnect** API as follows −

```
$rc = $dbh->disconnect  or warn $dbh->errstr;
```

The transaction behaviour of the disconnect method is, sadly, undefined. Some database systems (such as Oracle and Ingres) will automatically commit any outstanding changes, but others (such as Informix) will rollback any outstanding changes. Applications not using AutoCommit should explicitly call commit or rollback before calling disconnect.

Using NULL Values:

Undefined values, or undef, are used to indicate NULL values. You can insert and update columns with a NULL value as you would a non-NULL value. These examples insert and update the column age with a NULL value −

```
$sth = $dbh->prepare(qq {

    INSERT INTO TEST_TABLE (FIRST_NAME,
AGE) VALUES (?, ?)

    });
$sth->execute("Joe", undef);
```

Here **qq{}** is used to return a quoted string to **prepare** API. However, care must be taken when trying to use NULL values in a WHERE clause. Consider −

```
SELECT FIRST_NAME FROM TEST_TABLE WHERE
age = ?
```

Binding an undef (NULL) to the placeholder will not select rows, which have a NULL age! At least for database engines that conform to the SQL standard. Refer to the SQL manual for your database engine or any SQL book for the reasons for this. To explicitly select NULLs you have to say "WHERE age IS NULL".

A common issue is to have a code fragment handle a value that could be either defined or undef (non-NULL or NULL) at runtime. A simple technique is to prepare the appropriate statement as needed, and substitute the placeholder for non-NULL cases −

```
$sql_clause = defined $age? "age = ?" : "age IS NULL";
```

```
$sth = $dbh->prepare(qq {

    SELECT FIRST_NAME FROM TEST_TABLE
WHERE $sql_clause

    });

$sth->execute(defined $age ? $age : ());
```

Some Other DBI Functions:

available_drivers

```
@ary = DBI->available_drivers;

@ary = DBI->available_drivers($quiet);
```

Returns a list of all available drivers by searching for DBD::* modules through the directories in @INC. By default, a warning is given if some drivers are hidden by others of the same name in earlier directories. Passing a true value for $quiet will inhibit the warning.

installed_drivers

```
%drivers = DBI->installed_drivers();
```

Returns a list of driver name and driver handle pairs for all drivers 'installed' (loaded) into the current process. The driver name does not include the 'DBD::' prefix.

data_sources

```
@ary = DBI->data_sources($driver);
```

Returns a list of data sources (databases) available via the named driver. If $driver is empty or undef, then the value of the DBI_DRIVER environment variable is used.

quote

```
$sql = $dbh->quote($value);

$sql = $dbh->quote($value, $data_type);
```

Quote a string literal for use as a literal value in an SQL statement, by escaping any special characters (such as quotation marks) contained within the string and adding the required type of outer quotation marks.

```
$sql = sprintf "SELECT foo FROM bar WHERE baz = %s",

        $dbh->quote("Don't");
```

For most database types, quote would return 'Don''t' (including the outer quotation marks). It is valid for the quote() method to return an SQL expression that evaluates to the desired string. For example –

```
$quoted = $dbh->quote("one\ntwo\0three")
```

may produce results which will be equivalent to

CONCAT('one', CHAR(12), 'two', CHAR(0), 'three')

Methods Common to All Handles:

err

$rv = $h->err;

or

$rv = $DBI::err

or

$rv = $h->err

Returns the native database engine error code from the last driver method called. The code is typically an integer but you should not assume that. This is equivalent to $DBI::err or $h->err.

errstr

$str = $h->errstr;

or

```
$str = $DBI::errstr
```

or

```
$str = $h->errstr
```

Returns the native database engine error message from the last DBI method called. This has the same lifespan issues as the "err" method described above. This is equivalent to $DBI::errstr or $h->errstr.

rows

```
$rv = $h->rows;
```

or

```
$rv = $DBI::rows
```

This returns the number of rows effected by previous SQL statement and equivalent to $DBI::rows.

trace

```
$h->trace($trace_settings);
```

DBI sports an extremely useful ability to generate runtime tracing information of what it's doing, which can be a huge time-saver when trying to track down strange problems in your DBI programs. You can use different values to set trace level. These values varies from 0 to 4. The value 0 means disable trace and 4 means generate complete trace.

Interpolated Statements are Prohibited

It is highly recommended not to use interpolated statements as follows −

```
while ($first_name = <>) {

  my $sth = $dbh->prepare("SELECT *

              FROM TEST_TABLE

              WHERE FIRST_NAME = '$first_name'");

  $sth->execute();

  # and so on ...

}
```

Thus don't use interpolated statement instead use **bind value** to prepare dynamic SQL statement.

Perl - CGI Programming

What is CGI ?

- A Common Gateway Interface, or CGI, is a set of standards that defines how information is exchanged between the web server and a custom script.

- The CGI specs are currently maintained by the NCSA and NCSA defines CGI is as follows −

- *The Common Gateway Interface, or CGI, is a standard for external gateway programs to interface with information servers such as HTTP servers.*

- The current version is CGI/1.1 and CGI/1.2 is under progress.

Web Browsing

To understand the concept of CGI, lets see what happens when we click a hyper link available on a web page to browse a particular web page or URL.

- Your browser contacts web server using HTTP protocol and demands for the URL, i.e., web page filename.

- Web Server will check the URL and will look for the filename requested. If web server finds that file then it sends the file back to the browser without any further execution otherwise sends an error message indicating that you have requested a wrong file.

• Web browser takes response from web server and displays either the received file content or an error message in case file is not found.

However, it is possible to set up HTTP server in such a way so that whenever a file in a certain directory is requested that file is not sent back; instead it is executed as a program, and whatever that program outputs as a result, that is sent back for your browser to display. This can be done by using a special functionality available in the web server and it is called **Common Gateway Interface** or CGI and such programs which are executed by the server to produce final result, are called CGI scripts. These CGI programs can be a PERL Script, Shell Script, C or C++ program, etc.

CGI Architecture Diagram:

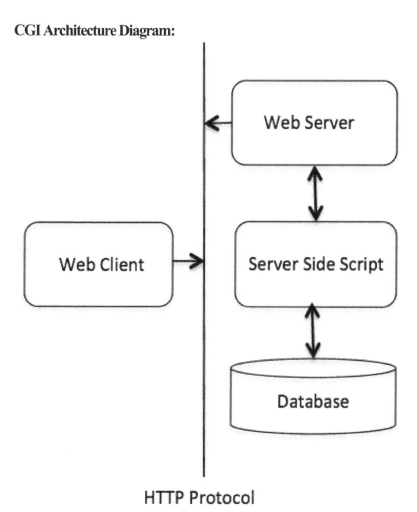

HTTP Protocol

Web Server Support and Configuration:

Before you proceed with CGI Programming, make sure that your Web Server supports CGI functionality and it is configured to handle CGI programs. All the CGI programs to be executed by the web server are kept in a preconfigured directory. This directory is called CGI directory and by convention it is named as /cgi-bin. By convention Perl CGI files will have extention as **.cgi**.

First CGI Program:

Before running your CGI program, make sure you have change mode of file using **chmod 755 hello.cgi** UNIX command.

```
#!/usr/bin/perl

print "Content-type:text/html\r\n\r\n";

print '<html>';

print '<head>';

print '<title>Hello Word - First CGI Program</title>';

print '</head>';

print '<body>';

print '<h2>Hello Word! This is my first CGI program</h2>';

print '</body>';

print '</html>';


1;
```

Now if you click **hello.cgi** link then request goes to web server who search for hello.cgi in /cgi-bin directory, execute it and whatever result got generated, web server sends that result back to the web browser, which is as follows –

Hello Word! This is my first CGI program

This hello.cgi script is a simple Perl script which is writing its output on STDOUT file, i.e., screen. There is one important and extra feature available which is first line to be printed **Content-type:text/html\r\n\r\n**. This line is sent back to the browser and specifies the content type to be displayed on the browser screen. Now you must have undertood basic concept of CGI and you can write many complicated CGI programs using Perl. This script can interact with any other exertnal system also to exchange information such as a database, web services, or any other complex interfaces.

Understanding HTTP Header:

The very first line **Content-type:text/html\r\n\r\n** is a part of HTTP header, which is sent to the browser so that browser can understand the incoming content from server side. All the HTTP header will be in the following form –

HTTP Field Name: Field Content

For Example –

Content-type:text/html\r\n\r\n

There are few other important HTTP headers, which you will use frequently in your CGI Programming.

Sr.No.	Header & Description
1	**Content-type: String** A MIME string defining the format of the content being returned. Example is Content-type:text/html
2	**Expires: Date String** The date when the information becomes invalid. This should be used by the browser to decide when a page needs to be refreshed. A valid date string should be in the format 01 Jan 1998 12:00:00 GMT.
3	**Location: URL String** The URL that should be returned instead of the URL requested. You can use this filed to redirect

	a request to any other location.
4	**Last-modified: String** The date of last modification of the file.
5	**Content-length: String** The length, in bytes, of the data being returned. The browser uses this value to report the estimated download time for a file.
6	**Set-Cookie: String** Set the cookie passed through the *string*

CGI Environment Variables:

All the CGI program will have access to the following environment variables. These variables play an important role while writing any CGI program.

Sr.No.	Variables Names & Description
1	**CONTENT_TYPE** The data type of the content. Used when the client is sending attached content to the server.

	For example file upload, etc.
2	**CONTENT_LENGTH** The length of the query information. It's available only for POST requests
3	**HTTP_COOKIE** Returns the set cookies in the form of key & value pair.
4	**HTTP_USER_AGENT** The User-Agent request-header field contains information about the user agent originating the request. Its name of the web browser.
5	**PATH_INFO** The path for the CGI script.
6	**QUERY_STRING** The URL-encoded information that is sent with GET method request.
7	**REMOTE_ADDR**

The IP address of the remote host making the request. This can be useful for logging or for authentication purpose.

8 | **REMOTE_HOST**

The fully qualified name of the host making the request. If this information is not available then REMOTE_ADDR can be used to get IR address.

9 | **REQUEST_METHOD**

The method used to make the request. The most common methods are GET and POST.

10 | **SCRIPT_FILENAME**

The full path to the CGI script.

11 | **SCRIPT_NAME**

The name of the CGI script.

12 | **SERVER_NAME**

The server's hostname or IP Address.

13 | **SERVER_SOFTWARE**

The name and version of the software the server is running.

Here is a small CGI program to list down all the CGI variables supported by your Web server.

```perl
#!/usr/bin/perl

print "Content-type: text/html\n\n";
print "<font size=+1>Environment</font>\n";
foreach (sort keys %ENV) {
  print "<b>$_</b>: $ENV{$_}<br>\n";
}

1;
```

Raise a "File Download" Dialog Box?

Sometime it is desired that you want to give option where a user will click a link and it will pop up a "File Download" dialogue box to the user instead of displaying actual content. This is very easy and will be achived through HTTP header.

This HTTP header will be different from the header mentioned in previous section. For example, if you want to make a **FileName**file downloadable from a given link then it's syntax will be as follows −

```perl
#!/usr/bin/perl


# HTTP Header

print   "Content-Type:application/octet-stream;   name   =
\"FileName\"\r\n";

print   "Content-Disposition:   attachment;   filename   =
\"FileName\"\r\n\n";


# Actual File Content will go hear.

open( FILE, "<FileName" );

while(read(FILE, $buffer, 100) ) {

  print("$buffer");

}
```

GET and POST Methods:

You must have come across many situations when you need to pass some information from your browser to the web server and ultimately to your CGI Program handling your requests. Most frequently browser uses two methods to pass this information to the web server. These methods are **GET** Method and **POST**Method. Let's check them one by one.

Passing Information using GET Method:

The GET method sends the encoded user information appended to the page URL itself. The page and the encoded information are separated by the ? character as follows –

http://www.test.com/cgi-bin/hello.cgi?key1=value1&key2=value2

The GET method is the defualt method to pass information from a browser to the web server and it produces a long string that appears in your browser's Location:box. You should never use GET method if you have password or other sensitive information to pass to the server. The GET method has size limitation: only 1024 characters can be passed in a request string.

This   information   is   passed using **QUERY_STRING** header and will be accessible in your   CGI   Program   through   QUERY_STRING environment variable which you can parse and use in your CGI program.

You can pass information by simply concatenating key and value pairs alongwith any URL or you can use HTML <FORM> tags to pass information using GET method.

Simple URL Example: Get Method

Below is **hello_get.cgi** script to handle input given by web browser.

```perl
#!/usr/bin/perl


local ($buffer, @pairs, $pair, $name, $value, %FORM);
# Read in text
$ENV{'REQUEST_METHOD'} =~ tr/a-z/A-Z/;
if ($ENV{'REQUEST_METHOD'} eq "GET") {
   $buffer = $ENV{'QUERY_STRING'};
}
# Split information into name/value pairs
@pairs = split(/&/, $buffer);
```

```perl
foreach $pair (@pairs) {
  ($name, $value) = split(/=/, $pair);
  $value =~ tr/+/ /;
  $value =~ s/%(..)/pack("C", hex($1))/eg;
  $FORM{$name} = $value;
}
$first_name = $FORM{first_name};
$last_name  = $FORM{last_name};
print "Content-type:text/html\r\n\r\n";
print "<html>";
print "<head>";
print "<title>Hello - Second CGI Program</title>";
print "</head>";
print "<body>";
print "<h2>Hello $first_name $last_name - Second CGI
Program</h2>";
print "</body>";
print "</html>";

1;
```

Simple FORM Example: GET Method

Here is a simple example, which passes two values using HTML FORM and submit button. We are going to use the same CGI script hello_get.cgi to handle this input.

```
<FORM action = "/cgi-bin/hello_get.cgi" method = "GET">

First Name: <input type = "text" name = "first_name">
<br>


Last Name: <input type = "text" name = "last_name">

<input type = "submit" value = "Submit">

</FORM>
```

Here is the actual output of the above form coding. Now you can enter First and Last Name and then click submit button to see the result.

First Name:

Last Name:

Submit

Passing Information using POST Method

A more reliable method of passing information to a CGI program is the **POST** method. This packages the information in exactly the same way as GET methods, but instead of sending it as a text string after a **?** in the URL, it sends it as a separate message as a part of HTTP header. Web server provides this message to the CGI script in the form of the standard input.

Below is the modified **hello_post.cgi** script to handle input given by the web browser. This script will handle GET as well as POST method.

```perl
#!/usr/bin/perl


local ($buffer, @pairs, $pair, $name, $value, %FORM);
# Read in text
$ENV{'REQUEST_METHOD'} =~ tr/a-z/A-Z/;
if ($ENV{'REQUEST_METHOD'} eq "POST") {
   read(STDIN, $buffer, $ENV{'CONTENT_LENGTH'});
} else {
   $buffer = $ENV{'QUERY_STRING'};
}
```

```perl
# Split information into name/value pairs
@pairs = split(/&/, $buffer);
foreach $pair (@pairs) {
  ($name, $value) = split(/=/, $pair);
  $value =~ tr/+/ /;
  $value =~ s/%(..)/pack("C", hex($1))/eg;
  $FORM{$name} = $value;
}
$first_name = $FORM{first_name};
$last_name  = $FORM{last_name};


print "Content-type:text/html\r\n\r\n";
print "<html>";
print "<head>";
print "<title>Hello - Second CGI Program</title>";
print "</head>";
print "<body>";
print "<h2>Hello $first_name $last_name - Second CGI Program</h2>";
print "</body>";
```

```
print "</html>";


1;
```

Let us take again same examle as above, which passes two values using HTML FORM and submit button. We are going to use CGI script hello_post.cgi to handle this input.

```
<FORM action = "/cgi-bin/hello_post.cgi" method = "POST">

First Name: <input type = "text" name = "first_name">
<br>


Last Name: <input type = "text" name = "last_name">


<input type = "submit" value = "Submit">
</FORM>
```

Here is the actual output of the above form coding, You enter First and Last Name and then click submit button to see the result.

First Name:

Last Name:

Submit

Passing Checkbox Data to CGI Program:

Checkboxes are used when more than one option is required to be selected. Here is an example HTML code for a form with two checkboxes.

```
<form action = "/cgi-bin/checkbox.cgi" method = "POST"
target = "_blank">

<input type = "checkbox" name = "maths" value = "on">
Maths

<input type = "checkbox" name = "physics" value = "on">
Physics

<input type = "submit" value = "Select Subject">

</form>
```

The result of this code is the following form –

☑ Maths ☑ Physics Select Subject

Below is **checkbox.cgi** script to handle input given by web browser for radio button.

```
#!/usr/bin/perl


local ($buffer, @pairs, $pair, $name, $value, %FORM);
```

```perl
# Read in text
$ENV{'REQUEST_METHOD'} =~ tr/a-z/A-Z/;
if ($ENV{'REQUEST_METHOD'} eq "POST") {
  read(STDIN, $buffer, $ENV{'CONTENT_LENGTH'});
} else {
  $buffer = $ENV{'QUERY_STRING'};
}
# Split information into name/value pairs
@pairs = split(/&/, $buffer);
foreach $pair (@pairs) {
  ($name, $value) = split(/=/, $pair);
  $value =~ tr/+/ /;
  $value =~ s/%(..)/pack("C", hex($1))/eg;
  $FORM{$name} = $value;
}
if( $FORM{maths} ) {
  $maths_flag ="ON";
} else {
  $maths_flag ="OFF";
```

```perl
}

if( $FORM{physics} ) {

  $physics_flag ="ON";

} else {

  $physics_flag ="OFF";

}


print "Content-type:text/html\r\n\r\n";

print "<html>";

print "<head>";

print "<title>Checkbox - Third CGI Program</title>";

print "</head>";

print "<body>";

print "<h2> CheckBox Maths is : $maths_flag</h2>";

print "<h2> CheckBox Physics is : $physics_flag</h2>";

print "</body>";

print "</html>";


1;
```

Passing Radio Button Data to CGI Program:

Radio Buttons are used when only one option is required to be selected. Here is an example HTML code for a form with two radio button –

```html
<form action = "/cgi-bin/radiobutton.cgi" method = "POST" target = "_blank">

<input type = "radio" name = "subject" value = "maths">
Maths

<input type = "radio" name = "subject" value = "physics">
Physics

<input type = "submit" value = "Select Subject">

</form>
```

The result of this code is the following form –

○ Maths ⦿ Physics [Select Subject]

Below is **radiobutton.cgi** script to handle input given by the web browser for radio button.

```perl
#!/usr/bin/perl


local ($buffer, @pairs, $pair, $name, $value, %FORM);
# Read in text
```

```perl
$ENV{'REQUEST_METHOD'} =~ tr/a-z/A-Z/;

if ($ENV{'REQUEST_METHOD'} eq "POST") {

  read(STDIN, $buffer, $ENV{'CONTENT_LENGTH'});

} else {

  $buffer = $ENV{'QUERY_STRING'};

}

# Split information into name/value pairs

@pairs = split(/&/, $buffer);

foreach $pair (@pairs) {

  ($name, $value) = split(/=/, $pair);

  $value =~ tr/+/ /;

  $value =~ s/%(..)/pack("C", hex($1))/eg;

  $FORM{$name} = $value;

}

$subject = $FORM{subject};


print "Content-type:text/html\r\n\r\n";

print "<html>";

print "<head>";
```

```
print "<title>Radio - Fourth CGI Program</title>";

print "</head>";

print "<body>";

print "<h2> Selected Subject is $subject</h2>";

print "</body>";

print "</html>";



1;
```

Passing Text Area Data to CGI Program:

A textarea element is used when multiline text has to be passed to the CGI Program. Here is an example HTML code for a form with a TEXTAREA box –

```
<form action = "/cgi-bin/textarea.cgi" method = "POST"
target = "_blank">

<textarea name = "textcontent" cols = 40 rows = 4>

Type your text here...

</textarea>

<input type = "submit" value = "Submit">

</form>
```

The result of this code is the following form –

Below is the **textarea.cgi** script to handle input given by the web browser.

```perl
#!/usr/bin/perl


local ($buffer, @pairs, $pair, $name, $value, %FORM);
# Read in text
$ENV{'REQUEST_METHOD'} =~ tr/a-z/A-Z/;
if ($ENV{'REQUEST_METHOD'} eq "POST") {
  read(STDIN, $buffer, $ENV{'CONTENT_LENGTH'});
} else {
  $buffer = $ENV{'QUERY_STRING'};
}
# Split information into name/value pairs
@pairs = split(/&/, $buffer);
foreach $pair (@pairs) {
```

```perl
   ($name, $value) = split(/=/, $pair);

   $value =~ tr/+/ /;

   $value =~ s/%(..)/pack("C", hex($1))/eg;

   $FORM{$name} = $value;

}

$text_content = $FORM{textcontent};


print "Content-type:text/html\r\n\r\n";

print "<html>";

print "<head>";

print "<title>Text Area - Fifth CGI Program</title>";

print "</head>";

print "<body>";

print "<h2> Entered Text Content is $text_content</h2>";

print "</body>";

print "</html>";


1;
```

Passing Drop Down Box Data to CGI Program:

A drop down box is used when we have many options available but only one or two will be selected. Here is example HTML code for a form with one drop down box

```
<form action = "/cgi-bin/dropdown.cgi" method = "POST"
target = "_blank">

<select name = "dropdown">

<option value = "Maths" selected>Maths</option>

<option value = "Physics">Physics</option>

</select>

<input type = "submit" value = "Submit">

</form>
```

The result of this code is the following form –

Below is the **dropdown.cgi** script to handle input given by web browser.

```
#!/usr/bin/perl


local ($buffer, @pairs, $pair, $name, $value, %FORM);
# Read in text
```

```perl
$ENV{'REQUEST_METHOD'} =~ tr/a-z/A-Z/;
if ($ENV{'REQUEST_METHOD'} eq "POST") {
  read(STDIN, $buffer, $ENV{'CONTENT_LENGTH'});
} else {
  $buffer = $ENV{'QUERY_STRING'};
}
# Split information into name/value pairs
@pairs = split(/&/, $buffer);
foreach $pair (@pairs) {
  ($name, $value) = split(/=/, $pair);
  $value =~ tr/+/ /;
  $value =~ s/%(..)/pack("C", hex($1))/eg;
  $FORM{$name} = $value;
}
$subject = $FORM{dropdown};


print "Content-type:text/html\r\n\r\n";
print "<html>";
print "<head>";
```

```
print "<title>Dropdown Box - Sixth CGI Program</title>";

print "</head>";

print "<body>";

print "<h2> Selected Subject is $subject</h2>";

print "</body>";

print "</html>";



1;
```

Using Cookies in CGI:

HTTP protocol is a stateless protocol. But for a commercial website it is required to maintain session information among different pages. For example one user registration ends after transactions which spans through many pages. But how to maintain user's session information across all the web pages?

In many situations, using cookies is the most efficient method of remembering and tracking preferences, purchases, commissions, and other information required for better visitor experience or site statistics.

How It Works:

Your server sends some data to the visitor's browser in the form of a cookie. The browser may accept the cookie. If it does, it is stored as a plain text record on the visitor's hard drive. Now, when the visitor arrives at another page on your site, the cookie is available for retrieval. Once retrieved, your server knows/remembers what was stored.

Cookies are a plain text data record of 5 variable-length fields –

- **Expires** – The date the cookie will expire. If this is blank, the cookie will expire when the visitor quits the browser.

- **Domain** – The domain name of your site.

- **Path** – The path to the directory or web page that set the cookie. This may be blank if you want to retrieve the cookie from any directory or page.

- **Secure** – If this field contains the word "secure" then the cookie may only be retrieved with a secure server. If this field is blank, no such restriction exists.

- **Name = Value** – Cookies are set and retrviewed in the form of key and value pairs.

Setting up Cookies

It is very easy to send cookies to browser. These cookies will be sent along with the HTTP Header. Assuming you want to set UserID and Password as cookies. So it will be done as follows –

```
#!/usr/bin/perl


print "Set-Cookie:UserID = XYZ;\n";

print "Set-Cookie:Password = XYZ123;\n";

print "Set-Cookie:Expires = Tuesday, 31-Dec-2007 23:12:40 GMT";\n";

print "Set-Cookie:Domain = www.Perl Tutorial;\n";

print "Set-Cookie:Path = /perl;\n";

print "Content-type:text/html\r\n\r\n";
..........Rest of the HTML Content goes here....
```

Here we used **Set-Cookie** HTTP header to set cookies. It is optional to set cookies attributes like Expires, Domain, and Path. It is important to note that cookies are set before sending magic line **"Content-type:text/html\r\n\r\n.**

Retrieving Cookies

It is very easy to retrieve all the set cookies. Cookies are stored in CGI environment variable HTTP_COOKIE and they will have following form.

key1 = value1;key2 = value2;key3 = value3....

Here is an example of how to retrieve cookies.

```perl
#!/usr/bin/perl
$rcvd_cookies = $ENV{'HTTP_COOKIE'};
@cookies = split /;/, $rcvd_cookies;
foreach $cookie ( @cookies ) {
   ($key, $val) = split(/=/, $cookie); # splits on the first =.
   $key =~ s/^\s+//;
   $val =~ s/^\s+//;
   $key =~ s/\s+$//;
   $val =~ s/\s+$//;
   if( $key eq "UserID" ) {
      $user_id = $val;
   } elsif($key eq "Password") {
      $password = $val;
```

```
    }

}

print "User ID  = $user_id\n";

print "Password = $password\n";
```

This will produce the following result, provided above cookies have been set before calling retrieval cookies script.

```
User ID = XYZ
Password = XYZ123
```

CGI Modules and Libraries

You will find many built-in modules over the internet which provides you direct functions to use in your CGI program. Following are the important once.

- CGI Module
- Berkeley cgi-lib.pl

Perl - Packages and Modules

What are Packages?

The **package** statement switches the current naming context to a specified namespace (symbol table). Thus –

- A package is a collection of code which lives in its own namespace.

- A namespace is a named collection of unique variable names (also called a symbol table).

- Namespaces prevent variable name collisions between packages.

- Packages enable the construction of modules which, when used, won't clobber variables and functions outside of the modules's own namespace.

- The package stays in effect until either another package statement is invoked, or until the end of the current block or file.

- You can explicitly refer to variables within a package using the :: package qualifier.

Following is an example having main and Foo packages in a file. Here special variable __PACKAGE__ has been used to print the package name.

```perl
#!/usr/bin/perl


# This is main package
$i = 1;

print "Package name : ", __PACKAGE__ , " $i\n";


package Foo;
# This is Foo package
$i = 10;

print "Package name : ", __PACKAGE__ , " $i\n";


package main;
# This is again main package
$i = 100;

print "Package name : ", __PACKAGE__ , " $i\n";
print "Package name : ", __PACKAGE__ , " $Foo::i\n";


1;
```

When above code is executed, it produces the following result –

```
Package name : main 1
Package name : Foo 10
Package name : main 100
Package name : main 10
```

BEGIN and END Blocks

You may define any number of code blocks named BEGIN and END, which act as constructors and destructors respectively.

```
BEGIN { ... }
END { ... }
BEGIN { ... }
END { ... }
```

- Every **BEGIN** block is executed after the perl script is loaded and compiled but before any other statement is executed.

- Every END block is executed just before the perl interpreter exits.

- The BEGIN and END blocks are particularly useful when creating Perl modules.

Following example shows its usage –

```perl
#!/usr/bin/perl


package Foo;
print "Begin and Block Demo\n";


BEGIN {
   print "This is BEGIN Block\n"
}


END {
   print "This is END Block\n"
}


1;
```

When above code is executed, it produces the following result –

```
This is BEGIN Block
Begin and Block Demo
This is END Block
```

What are Perl Modules?

A Perl module is a reusable package defined in a library file whose name is the same as the name of the package with a .pm as extension.

A Perl module file called **Foo.pm** might contain statements like this.

```perl
#!/usr/bin/perl

package Foo;
sub bar {
  print "Hello $_[0]\n"
}

sub blat {
  print "World $_[0]\n"
}
1;
```

Few important points about Perl modules

- The functions **require** and **use** will load a module.

- Both use the list of search paths in **@INC** to find the module.

- Both functions **require** and **use** call the **eval** function to process the code.

- The **1;** at the bottom causes eval to evaluate to TRUE (and thus not fail).

The Require Function

A module can be loaded by calling the **require** function as follows –

```
#!/usr/bin/perl


require Foo;


Foo::bar( "a" );
Foo::blat( "b" );
```

You must have noticed that the subroutine names must be fully qualified to call them. It would be nice to enable the subroutine **bar** and **blat** to be imported into our own namespace so we wouldn't have to use the Foo:: qualifier.

The Use Function

A module can be loaded by calling the **use** function.

```
#!/usr/bin/perl


use Foo;


bar( "a" );
blat( "b" );
```

Notice that we didn't have to fully qualify the package's function names. The **use** function will export a list of symbols from a module given a few added statements inside a module.

```
require Exporter;
@ISA = qw(Exporter);
```

Then, provide a list of symbols (scalars, lists, hashes, subroutines, etc) by filling the list variable named **@EXPORT**: For Example −

```
package Module;


require Exporter;
```

```
@ISA = qw(Exporter);

@EXPORT = qw(bar blat);


sub bar { print "Hello $_[0]\n" }

sub blat { print "World $_[0]\n" }

sub splat { print "Not $_[0]\n" }  # Not exported!


1;
```

Create the Perl Module Tree

When you are ready to ship your Perl module, then there is standard way of creating a Perl Module Tree. This is done using **h2xs** utility. This utility comes along with Perl. Here is the syntax to use h2xs −

```
$h2xs -AX -n  ModuleName
```

For example, if your module is available in **Person.pm** file, then simply issue the following command −

```
$h2xs -AX -n Person
```

This will produce the following result −

```
Writing Person/lib/Person.pm
```

```
Writing Person/Makefile.PL
Writing Person/README
Writing Person/t/Person.t
Writing Person/Changes
Writing Person/MANIFEST
```

Here is the descritpion of these options –

- **-A** omits the Autoloader code (best used by modules that define a large number of infrequently used subroutines).

- **-X** omits XS elements (eXternal Subroutine, where eXternal means external to Perl, i.e., C).

- **-n** specifies the name of the module.

So above command creates the following structure inside Person directory. Actual result is shown above.

- Changes

- Makefile.PL

- MANIFEST (contains the list of all files in the package)

- README

- t/ (test files)

- lib/ (Actual source code goes here

So finally, you **tar** this directory structure into a file Person.tar.gz and you can ship it. You will have to update

README file with the proper instructions. You can also provide some test examples files in t directory.

Installing Perl Module:

Download a Perl module in the form tar.gz file. Use the following sequence to install any Perl Module **Person.pm** which has been downloaded in as **Person.tar.gz** file.

```
tar xvfz Person.tar.gz
cd Person
perl Makefile.PL
make
make install
```

The Perl interpreter has a list of directories in which it searches for modules (global array @INC).

Perl - Process Management

You can use Perl in various ways to create new processes as per your requirements. This tutorial will list down few important and most frequently used methods of creating and managing Perl processes.

- You can use special variables **$$** or **$PROCESS_ID** to get current process ID.

- Every process created using any of the mentioned methods, maintains its own virtual environment with-in **%ENV** variable.

- The **exit()** function always exits just the child process which executes this function and the main process as a whole will not exit unless all running child-processes have exited.

- All open handles are dup()-ed in child-processes, so that closing any handles in one process does not affect the others.

Backstick Operator

This simplest way of executing any Unix command is by using backstick operator. You simply put your command inside the backstick operator, which will result in execution of the command and returns its result which can be stored as follows –

```perl
#!/usr/bin/perl

@files = `ls -l`;

foreach $file (@files) {

   print $file;

}

1;
```

When the above code is executed, it lists down all the files and directories available in the current directory −

```
drwxr-xr-x 3 root root 4096 Sep 14 06:46 9-14
drwxr-xr-x 4 root root 4096 Sep 13 07:54 android
-rw-r--r-- 1 root root  574 Sep 17 15:16 index.htm
drwxr-xr-x 3  544  401 4096 Jul  6 16:49 MIME-Lite-3.01
-rw-r--r-- 1 root root   71 Sep 17 15:16 test.pl
drwx------ 2 root root 4096 Sep 17 15:11 vAtrJdy
```

The system() Function

You can also use **system()** function to execute any Unix command, whose output will go to the output of the perl script. By default, it is the screen, i.e., STDOUT, but you can redirect it to any file by using redirection operator > −

```
#!/usr/bin/perl


system( "ls -l")



l;
```

When above code is executed, it lists down all the files
and directories available in the current directory –

```
drwxr-xr-x 3 root root 4096 Sep 14 06:46 9-14
drwxr-xr-x 4 root root 4096 Sep 13 07:54 android
-rw-r--r-- 1 root root  574 Sep 17 15:16 index.htm
drwxr-xr-x 3  544  401 4096 Jul  6 16:49 MIME-Lite-3.01
-rw-r--r-- 1 root root   71 Sep 17 15:16 test.pl
drwx------ 2 root root 4096 Sep 17 15:11 vAtrJdy
```

Be careful when your command contains shell
environmental variables like $PATH or $HOME. Try
following three scenarios –

```
#!/usr/bin/perl


$PATH = "I am Perl Variable";


system('echo $PATH');  # Treats $PATH as shell variable

system("echo $PATH");  # Treats $PATH as Perl variable
```

```
system("echo \$PATH"); # Escaping $ works.


1;
```

When above code is executed, it produces the following result depending on what is set in shell variable $PATH.

```
/usr/local/bin:/bin:/usr/bin:/usr/local/sbin:/usr/sbin:/sbin
I am Perl Variable
/usr/local/bin:/bin:/usr/bin:/usr/local/sbin:/usr/sbin:/sbin
```

The fork() Function:

Perl provides a **fork()** function that corresponds to the Unix system call of the same name. On most Unix-like platforms where the fork() system call is available, Perl's fork() simply calls it. On some platforms such as Windows where the fork() system call is not available, Perl can be built to emulate fork() at the interpreter level.

The fork() function is used to clone a current process. This call create a new process running the same program at the same point. It returns the child pid to the parent process, 0 to the child process, or undef if the fork is unsuccessful.

You can use **exec()** function within a process to launch the requested executable, which will be executed in a separate process area and exec() will wait for it to complete before exiting with the same exit status as that process.

```perl
#!/usr/bin/perl


if(!defined($pid = fork())) {

    # fork returned undef, so unsuccessful

    die "Cannot fork a child: $!";

} elsif ($pid == 0) {

    print "Printed by child process\n";

    exec("date") || die "can't exec date: $!";


} else {

    # fork returned 0 nor undef

    # so this branch is parent

    print "Printed by parent process\n";

    $ret = waitpid($pid, 0);

    print "Completed process id: $ret\n";


}


1;
```

When above code is executed, it produces the following result –

```
Printed by parent process
Printed by child process
Tue Sep 17 15:41:08 CDT 2013
Completed process id: 17777
```

The **wait()** and **waitpid()** can be passed as a pseudo-process ID returned by fork(). These calls will properly wait for the termination of the pseudo-process and return its status. If you fork without ever waiting on your children using **waitpid()**function, you will accumulate zombies. On Unix systems, you can avoid this by setting $SIG{CHLD} to "IGNORE" as follows –

```perl
#!/usr/bin/perl


local $SIG{CHLD} = "IGNORE";


if(!defined($pid = fork())) {

   # fork returned undef, so unsuccessful

   die "Cannot fork a child: $!";

} elsif ($pid == 0) {

   print "Printed by child process\n";
```

```perl
exec("date") || die "can't exec date: $!";



} else {

# fork returned 0 nor undef

# so this branch is parent

print "Printed by parent process\n";

$ret = waitpid($pid, 0);

print "Completed process id: $ret\n";



}



1;
```

When above code is executed, it produces the following result –

```
Printed by parent process
Printed by child process
Tue Sep 17 15:44:07 CDT 2013
Completed process id: -1
```

The kill() Function:

Perl **kill('KILL', (Process List))** function can be used to terminate a pseudo-process by passing it the ID returned by fork().

Note that using kill('KILL', (Process List)) on a pseudo-process() may typically cause memory leaks, because the thread that implements the pseudo-process does not get a chance to clean up its resources.

You can use **kill()** function to send any other signal to target processes, for example following will send SIGINT to a process IDs 104 and 102 −

```perl
#!/usr/bin/perl


kill('INT', 104, 102);


1;
```

Perl - Embedded Documentation

You can embed Pod (Plain Old Text) documentation in your Perl modules and scripts. Following is the rule to use embedded documentation in your Perl Code –

Start your documentation with an empty line, a =**head1**command at the beginning, and end it with a =**cut**

Perl will ignore the Pod text you entered in the code. Following is a simple example of using embedded documentation inside your Perl code –

```
#!/usr/bin/perl


print "Hello, World\n";


=head1 Hello, World Example
This example demonstrate very basic syntax of Perl.
=cut


print "Hello, Universe\n";
```

When above code is executed, it produces the following result –

```
Hello, World
Hello, Universe
```

If you're going to put your Pod at the end of the file, and you're using an __END__ or __DATA__ cut mark, make sure to put an empty line there before the first Pod command as follows, otherwise without an empty line before the =**head1**, many translators wouldn't have recognized the =**head1** as starting a Pod block.

```perl
#!/usr/bin/perl


print "Hello, World\n";


while(<DATA>) {

 print $_;

}


__END__


=head1 Hello, World Example

This example demonstrate very basic syntax of Perl.

print "Hello, Universe\n";
```

When above code is executed, it produces the following result –

Hello, World

=head1 Hello, World Example
This example demonstrate very basic syntax of Perl.
print "Hello, Universe\n";

Let's take one more example for the same code without reading DATA part −

```
#!/usr/bin/perl


print "Hello, World\n";


__END__


=head1 Hello, World Example
```

This example demonstrate very basic syntax of Perl.

print "Hello, Universe\n";

When above code is executed, it produces the following result −

Hello, World

What is POD?

Pod is a simple-to-use markup language used for writing documentation for Perl, Perl programs, and Perl modules. There are various translators available for converting Pod to various formats like plain text, HTML, man pages, and more. Pod markup consists of three basic kinds of paragraphs –

- **Ordinary Paragraph** – You can use formatting codes in ordinary paragraphs, for bold, italic, code-style , hyperlinks, and more.

- **Verbatim Paragraph** – Verbatim paragraphs are usually used for presenting a codeblock or other text which does not require any special parsing or formatting, and which shouldn't be wrapped.

- **Command Paragraph** – A command paragraph is used for special treatment of whole chunks of text, usually as headings or parts of lists. All command paragraphs start with =, followed by an identifier, followed by arbitrary text that the command can use however it pleases. Currently recognized commands are –

```
=pod
=head1 Heading Text
=head2 Heading Text
```

```
=head3 Heading Text
=head4 Heading Text
=over indentlevel
=item stuff
=back
=begin format
=end format
=for format text...
=encoding type
=cut
```

POD Examples

Consider the following POD –

```
=head1 SYNOPSIS

Copyright 2019 [NEXCOD].

=cut
```

You can use **pod2html** utility available on Linux to convert above POD into HTML, so it will produce following result –

Copyright 2019 [NEXCOD].

Next, consider the following example –

```
=head2 An Example List


=over 4
```

```
=item * This is a bulleted list.

=item * Here's another item.

=back

=begin html

<p>

Here's some embedded HTML.  In this block I can

include images, apply <span style="color: green">

styles</span>, or do anything else I can do with

HTML.  pod parsers that aren't outputting HTML will

completely ignore it.

</p>

=end html
```

When you convert the above POD into HTML using pod2html, it will produce the following result –

```
An Example List
   This is a bulleted list.
   Here's another item.
Here's some embedded HTML. In this block I can include
images, apply
styles, or do anything else I can do with HTML. pod
parsers that aren't
outputting HTML will completely ignore it.
```

Thank You!

www.ingramcontent.com/pod-product-compliance
Lightning Source LLC
Chambersburg PA
CBHW031217050326
40689CB00009B/1364